FROM COLLEGE TO CAREER SECOND EDITION

WINNING RÉSUMÉS FOR COLLEGE GRADUATES

by
NANCY SCHUMAN
Vice President
Marketing & Operations
Career Blazers Personnel Services, Inc.
New York City

and

ADELE LEWIS
Former President and Founder
Career Blazers Agency, Inc.
New York City

BARRON'S

DEDICATION...

In memory of Anna Markart and Leah Lewis.

ACKNOWLEDGMENTS...

The authors would like to thank the following people for
their contributions to this book:
- Susan DeMuro
- George Gruber
- Ellen Schechterman
- Grace Schuman
- The Permanent Placement Division of Career Blazers Agency of
  New York City.

© 1993 by Barron's Educational Series, Inc.
Adapted from BETTER RESUMES FOR COLLEGE GRADUATES
© Copyright 1985 by Barron's Educational Series, Inc.

All inquiries should be addressed to:
Barron's Educational Series, Inc.
250 Wireless Boulevard
Hauppauge, New York 11788

Library of Congress Catalog Card No. 92-37081

International Standard Book No. 0-8120-1433-2

Library of Congress Cataloging-in-Publication Data
Schuman, Nancy
    From college to career—: winning resumes for college graduates / by Nancy
Schuman, Adele Lewis.
        p.   cm.
    Adapted from: Better resumes for college graduates / by Adele Lewis.
    ISBN 0-8120-1433-2
    1. Résumés (Employment)   2. College graduates—Employment.   I. Lewis, Adele
Beatrice, 1927–1990. Better resumes for college graduates.   II. Title.
HF5383.S328 1993
650.14—dc20
                                                                        92-37081
                                                                        CIP

PRINTED IN THE UNITED STATES OF AMERICA

3456 100 987654321

CONTENTS

INTRODUCTION

There is no feeling so devastating as the one that comes after a hard day of making the employment-agency rounds, dropping into the personnel departments of companies you'd love to work at—and still no decent job offer in sight. On the other hand, there is no feeling quite as exhilarating and triumphant as looking for a job and receiving several offers. For recent college graduates, as well as for those high on the corporate ladder, looking for a job can be either a triumph or a catastrophe, depending on one's expertise in the art of job hunting.

From long years of experience working with college graduates seeking entry-level jobs, we've come to understand that the looking for and the getting of a job is a skill. It is a skill that can be learned, and once acquired it will become a lifetime asset and forever remove any trepidation in regard to the job hunt.

We believe the college graduate looking for an entry level job should aim for the best available, trying to avoid settling for less. But ambition must be tempered with a realistic attitude, evaluating each opportunity with a flexible and farsighted view. Examine each offer with such questions as "What can I learn?" "Is it promotable?" "Can I add something to that job which will make it more important to the company?" and "How will it look on my résumé?"

Be very careful not to be fooled by job titles. A secretary to an editor may very well be an editorial assistant or editorial trainee; a gal/guy Friday position in an advertising agency might really be the entry to a copywriting spot; "secretary to an executive" might be another name for an administrative assistant; a sales position can often be the stepping-stone to a marketing or management career. In essence, we're pointing out that not only jobs labeled *trainee* have potential.

It really is true that companies prefer to train their own staff and promote from within. We've placed "secretaries" who have become editors, publishers, account executives, television producers, production managers, writers, researchers, office managers, administrators, and vice presidents.

Though we believe in holding out for the very best, we are also aware that a job is often what you make of it. We also believe that proximity is the mother of opportunity, so that an entry position in the field of your choice may very well be the first step to a successful career.

It is extremely important for the job seeker to maintain an optimistic, confident point of view. No matter what the economy, there are always jobs to be filled and companies that are recruiting. If this were not so, the more than 5,000 employment agencies currently doing business in the United States would have to close their doors. In bad times as well as good, some of the vast majority of the employed retire, others relocate, others leave for personal reasons. Each time this happens, another job-to-be-filled opens. Our changing technology creates thousands of jobs that didn't exist twenty years ago, and even the fact that our population has a longer life span accounts for an increasing number of positions to be filled.

It is true that in times of an economic recession the recent college grad might have to try a little harder, but if he or she is willing to sustain an honest effort, possibly make certain compromises, and in some cases gain additional skills, the job hunt properly done is bound to be successful. Even in "bad" times a successful job campaign often results in several offers, and the problem changes from "How do I find a job?" to "Which job do I take?"

KYOCERA
F-1000 A

LISTING OF SAMPLE RESUMES BY MAJOR:

- ❏ Accounting
- ❏ American Studies
- ❏ Anthropology/Sociology
- ❏ Architecture
- ❏ Art History
- ❏ Behavioral Science
- ❏ Biology
- ❏ Broadcast Communications
- ❏ Business Administration
- ❏ Chemistry
- ❏ Communications
- ❏ Communications
- ❏ Communications/Public Relations
- ❏ Computers
- ❏ Computers
- ❏ Creative Writing
- ❏ Criminal Justice
- ❏ Drama/Dance
- ❏ East Asian Studies
- ❏ Economics
- ❏ Economics
- ❏ Education
- ❏ Electronic Journalism
- ❏ Engineering/Civil
- ❏ Engineering/Electrical
- ❏ English
- ❏ Environmental Design
- ❏ European/Art History
- ❏ Fashion Studies
- ❏ Finance/MBA
- ❏ Fine Arts
- ❏ Foreign Language/Spanish
- ❏ Geography/Geology
- ❏ Government
- ❏ History
- ❏ Hotel & Restaurant Admin.
- ❏ Human Resources Management
- ❏ Illustration/Photography
- ❏ Industrial & Labor Relations
- ❏ International Studies
- ❏ Journalism
- ❏ Journalism
- ❏ Languages
- ❏ Law
- ❏ Law
- ❏ Legal Studies/Paralegal
- ❏ Liberal Arts
- ❏ Liberal Arts
- ❏ Management Information Systems
- ❏ Marketing
- ❏ Marketing/Consumer Behavior
- ❏ Mathematics
- ❏ Medieval & Renaissance Studies
- ❏ Metropolitan Studies
- ❏ Music
- ❏ Music Performance
- ❏ Nursing
- ❏ Nutrition
- ❏ Paralegal
- ❏ Personnel
- ❏ Philosophy
- ❏ Physical Therapy
- ❏ Political Science
- ❏ Psychology
- ❏ Public Administration
- ❏ Public Health/Biology
- ❏ Radio/Television/Film
- ❏ Social Work
- ❏ Sociology
- ❏ Special Education
- ❏ Speech Communication
- ❏ Sports Administration/ Physical Education
- ❏ Telecommunications
- ❏ Textile Design

Résumés begin on page 41.

1

THE PERFECT JOB FOR YOU

The very first step in finding that "perfect" entry-level job is getting to know what you are looking for. Knowing where your talents lie, what you enjoy doing, and how that can be translated into a job title is the very guts of a successful job campaign. Knowledge of the job market, a dynamic résumé, superior contacts in the business world—all great assests in a job campaign—will not help you if you are basically unaware of your real interests and motivations.

Recent college graduates (especially those with a major in liberal arts) are surprisingly unsophisticated about the nature of entry-level jobs and very often extremely naïve when asked, "What kind of job are you looking for?" A graduate with a degree in engineering is quite certain he or she is looking for an entry-level engineering job; likewise an accounting major is very straightforward in seeking a position in the accounting field. But those with majors in the humanities or liberal arts are not always quite sure where they fit in.

It is well worth the effort to spend a little time analyzing the inner you—discovering the situations in which you are the happiest, being aware of exactly what turns you on. Socrates said the basis of wisdom is self-knowledge, and from that awareness all other knowledge can be acquired. It is obvious that it's impossible to understand anything until you understand yourself.

To enable you to better understand how your characteristics, interests, and needs can help you choose the most suitable job, we've prepared an informal inventory which includes a personality profile and a working conditions inventory (see pages 3 and 4). If you spend some time with this inventory, it will definitely help you to pinpoint your career direction.

ADJECTIVES DESCRIBE YOU

To help you evaluate some of your personality traits, we have prepared a short list of adjectives. Simply circle those qualities that seem best to describe you. It is interesting to ask a friend or relative to choose the characteristics that he or she thinks best represent you. Analyze both sets of responses. You may be surprised to see the difference between how you perceive yourself and how others do.

When you have completed the checklist, analyze your responses in relationship to the descriptions of personality traits that are found in various fields.

independent	curious	easygoing
agreeable	sensitive	self-possessed
adaptable	tactful	quiet
abrupt	attractive	reserved
accommodating	poised	conservative
accepting	polished	chance-taker
administrative	impatient	gentle
altruistic	literate	follower
argumentative	energetic	leader
unassuming	shy	patient
businesslike	forceful	loner
relaxed	aggressive	orderly
professional	reliable	diplomatic
uncooperative	quick-tempered	flippant
dedicated	avid reader	do-gooder
fashion-minded	money-oriented	realistic
resourceful	bookish	humane
tenacious	high-energy	sensitive
extrovert	introvert	perfectionist
discreet	helpful	insightful
well-dressed	ambitious	moody
polished	important	cheerful
bad-tempered	confident	fast-thinking
competitive	sympathetic	fast-talking
informal	empathetic	happy
artistic	serious	kind
logical	disciplined	bored
creative	good listener	hostile
honest	literary	irritable
unpleasant	lazy	conscientious

If you have personality traits that fall into the grouping of easygoing, tactful, serious, reliable, or businesslike, you will fit into almost any field or industry. You will be an excellent candidate for a management trainee in a Fortune 500 corporation as well as in either a small or medium-size company.

If, along with those traits, you find that you circled traits that cluster around such characteristics as ambitious, money-oriented, forceful, energetic, aggressive, high-energy, creative, competitive, confident, or self-possessed, you'd be happy and successful in such fields as advertising, public relations, marketing, sales, publicity, or communications. Bear in mind that most large companies have their own marketing, advertising, and public relations departments, so you're not limited to only agency positions. If you find the adjectives that best describe you cluster around such traits as kind, insightful, humane, sympathetic, tactful, conscientious, empathetic, good listener, helpful, and patient, it is very likely you'll find your niche in such areas as social services, personnel, or any of the growing health-care fields.

Such traits as patient, orderly, logical, perfectionist, curious, introverted, quiet, and serious are among those shared by people successful in fields such as paralegal research, market research, libraries, education, copy editing, or specific areas of the computer industry.

Those who find that their traits fall into groups such as well-dressed, extroverted, fashion-minded, or polished should investigate jobs in the retailing, textile, or cosmetic industries.

Publishing (books, magazines, trade journals, and newspapers) is a good choice for those whose traits include literary, bookish, realistic, or tenacious. However, most college graduates are very naïve about the publishing field—they imagine it to be an area of great creativity, dedicated to the search for great literature. Be aware that publishing is a business, and like any other business, its primary goal is to make a profit, often rejecting a scholarly manuscript while paying a large advance for a work of lesser quality that might become a best seller. The recent graduate often makes a mistake in thinking of "editorial" as the only area in publishing that is career-oriented—there are also tremendous opportunities in book sales, publicity, subsidiary rights, and production.

As you probably noted, there are a number of what could be termed negative characteristics listed in this informal inventory. Although none of us is perfect and everyone has a periodic bad day, such traits as hostility, impatience, and moodiness tend to work against you both in getting a job and in being promoted. If you find you have circled more than five of these characteristics, you might discuss these feelings with a counselor.

TAKE A PERSONAL INVENTORY

We've prepared a few questions which, if considered carefully, will give you more insight into your preferences and will help you in career evaluations. A space is provided for your answer to the right of the questions.

Your Deepest Feelings   **Yes**   **No**

1. I find I spend most of my leisure time in the evenings with friends rather than reading or pursuing some hobby or craft.
2. I can be "turned on" by meeting new people and immediately feel comfortable.
3. I can be "turned down" (take rejection) without being upset.
4. I enjoy being in a competitive situation.
5. I am a self-starter and like taking control over my destiny.
6. In a group, I'm usually the person to initiate group activities.

7. I am well motivated and I enjoy motivating other people.
8. I like to take charge and persuade people to do things my way.
9. I believe the pursuit of money is a realistic end in itself.

Your Fundamental Philosophy   Yes   No

1. I'm the type of person who is happiest when being of service to others.
2. I either have done or would be interested in doing volunteer work with physically or emotionally ill people.
3. People often come to me with their problems and I enjoy helping them find solutions.
4. I believe my work should somehow contribute to the betterment of society.
5. I am comfortable with senior citizens as well as with my own age group.
6. I enjoy meeting new people.
7. I can be with people with severe problems and still maintain my equilibrium and not become depressed.
8. I feel that I have a lot of compassion.
9. I'm the sort of person who needs to be needed.
10. I'm responsive to other people and their needs.

Your Preferred Working Conditions   Yes   No

1. I much prefer to spend a quiet evening reading, sewing, building models, or pursuing a hobby than being with a group of people.
2. I feel I need a lot of privacy and enjoy being alone.
3. I would rather work independently than as part of a team.
4. I find I'm more productive when there is little or no pressure.
5. I feel I work most effectively in a steady, even-paced environment.
6. I like to know exactly what my workday will be like; in other words, I like to do the same things every day.
7. Doing the same thing every day would bore me. I like a variety of challenges.

Your Preferred Physical Surroundings   **Yes**   **No**

1. I am happiest in a restricted area, i.e., office, lab, classroom.
2. I much prefer to work outdoors.
3. I need to avoid places where people smoke.
4. I like to work near home and not have a lengthy commute each day.
5. I prefer the quiet time on the train, commuting to work.
6. I must work where it is very quiet.
7. I work better when there's lots going on around me.

If most of you answer "yes" to most of the statements in the first list (Your Deepest Feelings) you will be very successful in those fields requiring leadership qualities and where there is a strong focus on financial gain. We suggest you slant your job campaign to the following industries:

Advertising
Business
Communications (Advertising, Publishing, Public Relations, Television)
Insurance
Finance (Investments, Banking)
Manufacturing
International Trade
Sales
Real Estate

If, on the other hand, you found that the statements in the second group were more "you," you would probably more likely fulfill your needs in one of those fields dedicated to a better world, such as:

Social Science
Teaching
Rehabilitation
Health
Social Service
Clergy
Fund Raising
Foundations
Therapy and Counseling

The third set poses a very fundamental approach to how you perceive both pressure and variety. Pressure, to those who act badly to it, can produce a very unhealthy, stressful state. On the other hand, "one man's meat can be another man's poison," and those who are stimulated by working against the odds, who thrive on pressure, can find working in a quiet, steady atmosphere cause for a rise in their blood pressure.

Those who answered "yes" to most of the statements in the third group will be happier in a nonpressure, steady-paced working atmosphere. Generally, these jobs can be found in such fields as:

Libraries
Physical Sciences
Computer and Related Occupations
Insurance
Research
Banking

Conversely, those who answered "no" to the brief sentences in group 3 are motivated by pressure and should pursue careers in the following areas:

Business
Communications (Advertising, Publishing, Public Relations, Television)
Sales
Science Industries
Retailing

The physical surroundings you prefer actually break down to either an inside or an outside job, although other considerations such as convenience, ambiance, and comfort also come into play.

If you're happiest working indoors, you will find the majority of fields have definite space allocations. However, if you consider the atmosphere of the workplace an important factor in your decision of which job to take, and you find the decor of a given company irritating, it is very likely that you will be uncomfortable and unable to give that company your all.

For those of you opposed to working in a closed-in area, several fields offer possibilities:

Coaching (Athletics)
Archeology
Sales
Forestry
Landscape Architecture
Performing Arts
Law Enforcement

WHERE THE JOBS ARE

One of the biggest problems many liberal arts majors face is how to turn their academic knowledge into business skills. Very few openings are tailored for the graduating English major, whose college experiences have involved literary criticism and research. But these experiences have developed skills that can be applied successfully to certain fields. Advertising agencies, for example, may not be interested in the English major's knowledge of Chaucer, but they will like the way that major puts thoughts down on paper. Likewise, anthropology majors may at graduation be intellectually involved in the development of early humankind, but that understanding of people and their motivations can be applied very nicely to market research or to the problems of personnel management at a large corporation.

The trick is knowing in which fields a major is most likely to apply best. The general intellectual development you have gained from your education can be applied to all types of work, but you will have an easier time getting that foot in the door if you head directly to certain industries or businesses. The following is a listing of suggested fields of work, matched to the college majors that are most popular today. Obviously we have omitted business majors from this listing because there is a far more direct correlation with the business world.

Art/Art History Major

Jobs consist of commercial art work, receptionists, selling art objects, and secretarial. Try:

- art departments of advertising agencies
- book production
- art galleries, fine graphic arts houses
- museums
- libraries

Communications/Broadcasting/Speech Major

Jobs can include production, script writing, film editing, collecting of props. Try:

- radio and television stations, radio and television packaging firms, cable companies
- film producers
- departments within educational organizations
- video producers
- industrial training groups/production houses
- trade associations
- nonprofit organizations

English Major

(also Journalism, English Literature, American Studies, Writing, Philosophy). Try:

- Publishing, including books, magazines (both trade and consumer), house organs, newspapers, etc.)
- Advertising, including copy departments of agencies, advertising departments of industry—writing brochures, catalogues, space ads, television scripts, continuity copy, promotional literature, direct mail, etc.
- Public Relations: agencies, nonprofit organizations, fund raisers, press releases, feature articles, brochures, pamphlets, etc.

- Industry: management trainee, sales, marketing
- Corporate Communications: manual/policy development, employee relations

Government/Political Science Major

The fortunate ones will be attending U.N. sessions writing speeches, releases, and features. There are a few openings with the various publications and organizations involved in international and national affairs. Also try:

- international affairs, history educational foundations
- diplomatic services, embassies
- trade associations and lobbying groups

Language Major

A few hard-to-get translation jobs in publishing. Try:

- international export, banking, industry
- specialized schools, diplomatic services, United Nations, embassies,
- import-export firms
- hotels, travel/tourism
- corporations with international offices

Music Major

Try:

- music publishers, record companies
- music departments of television in both studios and advertising agencies
- TV commercials
- community special events
- back offices of community orchestras, opera companies, etc.

Math Major

Jobs generally consist of trainee positions working with statistics, analyses, computing, business trends, etc. Try:

- insurance, banking, investment companies, market research, media departments
- advertising agencies, programming, management consultants
- research for industry and nonprofit organizations

Psychology/Sociology/Anthropology Major

Jobs generally cover statistical analysis, questionnaire research and case workers. Youth work covers programming, recreation, and administration. Also management and sales. Try:

- market research, personnel
- market research department of advertising agencies, social work, youth work

2
THE CURRENT JOB MARKET

One day the stock market is up, the next day it's down. Is the recession over? Is it beginning again? Is the economy really getting better? Everything (the gross national product, interest rates, employment figures) seems to indicate that the recession has hit bottom and we are going into a period of better economic conditions. This will mean an increase in hiring, more job openings, and less trauma in finding the perfect job for you.

However, you must realize that whether the economy is booming or sluggish, there are always job openings. Companies are forever recruiting. Some employees are promoted, others are transferred or retired, and, in consequence, staff vacancies are created and someone must be hired to fill them. Budget-minded companies often hire recent college graduates at less money than experienced people who will demand higher salaries.

HOW TO GET INFORMATION

The U.S. Department of Labor offers many publications that are extremely useful to the job seeker. We recommend that you glance through "The U.S. Department of Labor Statistics," which surveys every job category discussing educational requirements, the employment outlook, and the salary ranges being offered.

"The Job Outlook in Brief" in the *Occupational Outlook Quarterly* lists those jobs that will show the fastest growth. The Department of Labor reports some very interesting facts to the job seeker. It's worthwhile to spend some time studying it and try to use the information to your advantage.

On page 10 you will find a chart published in the *Occupational Outlook Quarterly* showing the average 1989 weekly salaries (before tax deductions) in a variety of fields. These figures include overtime, commissions or tips. They relate only to earnings from salaries or wages, and not to those people who are self-employed. Usually the earning power of the self-employed is higher in any occupation than that of the salaried worker. That is why physicians, who are generally self-employed and enjoy the highest income of all the occupations, are listed in the sixth position. That figure, $792, is the average of only those doctors who work for someone else.

These figures represent average earnings—that is, salaries of new graduates are included along with wages of the highly experienced—so the earnings of each occupation may seem low. Remember, too, that the span of income in a single occupation can be very broad.

WEEKLY EARNINGS IN OCCUPATIONS WITH EMPLOYMENT OF 50,000 OR MORE FOR AT LEAST 6 YEARS, 1983–1989

Occupation	1989 Median	Occupation	1989 Median
Lawyers	$900	Securities and financial service sales workers	$651
Airline pilots and navigators	807	Purchasing managers	651
Chemical engineers	807	Chemists, except biochemists	633
Electrical and electronics engineers	803	Structural metal workers	625
Aerospace engineers	801	Computer programmers	606
Physicians	792		
Engineers	775		
Mechanical engineers	766	Managers, medicine and health	604
Engineers	761	Telephone line installers and repairers	602
Managers: marketing, advertising, and public relations	753	Counselors, educational and vocational	598
		Tool and die makers	593
Pharmacists	748	Managers and administrators	589
Civil engineers	735	Administrators and officers, public administration	585
Administrators, education and related fields	712	Telephone installers and repairers	583
Computer systems analysts and scientists	711	Public relations specialists	576
		Supervisors, mechanics, and repairers	576
Teachers, college and university	711	Biological and life scientists	572
Industrial engineers	710		
Economists	704	Supervisors, construction occupations	569
Locomotive operating occupations	696	Registered nurses	569
Management analysts	693	Data processing equipment repairers	565
Post-secondary teachers, subject not specified	676	Sales representatives, commodities except retail, including sales engineers	561
		Electrical power installers and repairers	556
Supervisors, police and detective	674	Extractive occupations	555
Personnel and labor relations managers	668	Police and detectives, public service	554
Financial managers	667	Stationary engineers	554
Architects	667	Personnel, training, and labor relations specialists	552
Operations systems researchers and analysts	662		

Source: *Occupational Outlook Quarterly*, Fall 1990

MARKETING YOURSELF

Before you begin writing your résumé and undertaking the job search process, you need to understand two important facts:

1. Looking for a job IS a job!
2. Everything you do, say, or write about yourself must be self-promoting.

Fact #1: Looking for a job IS a job!

Many recent college grads (as well as job seekers of all backgrounds and experience levels) find the process of looking for a job exhausting. It is. It will take self-discipline, creativity, common sense, and perseverance. For every one interview you land, you'll receive twenty turndowns. Understand that you can't fit job hunting in between social engagements—it's much too serious. Your undergraduate career is over and now it's time to put your talents and education to work. We encourage you to utilize all the resources you have available to you: a network of friends and family, help-wanted advertisements, employment agencies and temporary help services, college placement offices and, of course, your own research and hard work.

Job hunting will require that you maintain a positive state of mind. You must be prepared to continuously psych yourself up for the challenge. Imagine that job hunting is akin to your most difficult college course and you won't settle for anything less than an "A." Your first post-college job doesn't have to last a lifetime, but how you feel about it will certainly have some impact on your self-esteem, your opportunity to grow, and your ambitions for the future.

As of right now, begin assuming a more "professional" role. You must successfully make the transition from student to employee, and this change must be apparent to anyone who interviews you for a position with his/her organization. You'll need to be organized, articulate and well groomed. Here are a few good techniques to help you get your job search off on the right foot.

- Read trade periodicals. If you don't already know which employers lead the field, start educating yourself about your proposed industry.
- Add a general business publication to your daily reading list to stay abreast of current events. Good choices include a big-city daily in your geographic area, *The New York Times*, *The Wall Street Journal*, or *USA Today*.
- Stay organized by using a pocket calendar. Write down all appointments—never rely on your memory, no matter how good it is.
- Make a habit of being on time for meetings. Better still, be 10 minutes early.
- Review your wardrobe. Can it survive a more corporate environment or is it strictly campus wear? Invest in more "grown up" attire.
- Develop a game plan for yourself. Job hunting shouldn't simply be hit or miss. Target a specific list of fifty employers and work at getting interviews at a minimum of five of these organizations.

Fact #2: Everything you do, say, or write about yourself must be self-promoting.

Job hunting makes all of us sales people. That doesn't mean we're seeking a career in sales; it does mean that you should think of yourself as the product and a prospective employer as the buyer. What do you do when you're thinking of making a big purchase? Do you read literature about a product line or examine the packaging? Well, employers do the same thing, only the promotional literature they review is in the form of a résumé...yours! Everyone wants to buy the highest-quality product available in his/her price range. Your own marketing campaign must convince an employer that you're "top of the line" material.

Your résumé will be a representation of you. It will say to an employer, "This is who I am; this is what I have done" and it will suggest what you are capable of doing. In the current marketplace, employers have the luxury of being selective, so by taking the time to develop an effective résumé and packaging it with an appealing cover letter, you are preparing a kind of print advertisement for yourself. A résumé will never ever, ever get you the job. It has a single goal; to get you the interview. However, a bad résumé (one that is poorly designed, filled with typos or scattered with grammatical errors) will surely *not* get you the job.

All of your contact with a potential employer must be cordial and professional. Your manner on the phone, the way you address your correspondence and format a letter, the way you shake hands, how you conduct yourself on an interview—all of this is self-promotion. Every job hunter needs to keep reminding him/herself that employers are "shopping" and, until you receive a job offer, you can't afford to look like shoddy goods.

3

YOUR RESUME

Your number one assignment, and perhaps the most difficult task facing you in your job campaign, is the preparation of your résumé.

When you consider that the average employer spends no more than thirty seconds skimming each résumé, it becomes apparent that yours must *stand out*—it has to be superior to the others that represent your competition. It is imperative that it be easy to read, that the facts be prominent and convincing, and that it incite enough interest to result in an interview.

Of course a résumé, no matter how cleverly written, can never reveal the many facets that make the total you—your talents, abilities, special skills, hopes, and aspirations. If your two-dimensional résumé cannot possibly duplicate the three-dimensional you, then exactly what is its purpose? In this complex, sophisticated world where time, distance, and sheer numbers of individuals work against personal involvement between employee and employer, the résumé has been adopted as a facsimile of you. Because it must represent you and interest the potential employer enough to want to see you, it has become very important—indeed, it is a vital document.

Think of your résumé as your personal dossier, your proxy, your statement of self—in other words, that which represents you. You must keep in mind that your résumé will be seen by many people involved in the hiring process, and each will examine it, judge it, and decide on this basis whether to invite you for an interview or whether it is a candidate, like so many others, to be simply discarded.

It is also helpful to think of your résumé as an advertisement—an advertisement whose product is *you!* We all recognize an ad that sells: it is brief, it contains strong facts, and those facts are prominent, convincing, and easy to read.

Writing your résumé will take time and much thought, but once you are aware of the logic involved in its preparation, we can guarantee that you'll not only have the ability to write a job-getting résumé, but you'll find a great deal of satisfaction in acquiring a new skill.

HOW LONG SHOULD A RESUME BE?

Résumés come in all sizes (we've received scraps of paper, 3″ × 5″ cards, and ten- to fifteen-page autobiographies), yet there is just one *correct* size—regular 8½″ × 11″. It is easily filed and easily handled, and it adds a professional touch.

A recent college graduate hasn't yet had enough experience to warrant more than one page. Anything longer is a tip-off that you are unable to make a judgment on the difference between the important facts and what might be considered unnecessary information.

It is the function of the résumé to describe and identify its writer in the most positive manner. Though every résumé—like every individual—is different, all must contain the following information:

1. Your name, address, and phone number. If you're sending out résumés while still in college, it is wise to give the phone number where you can be reached after you have graduated. In your cover letter, be sure to mention when you will be available for interviews.
2. Educational history: Name and address of college and which degree received. (If you maintained an average of 3.0 out of 4.0, that's something to be proud of—*be sure* that it is mentioned in your résumé. On the other hand, if you barely graduated or maintained a consistently low average, don't include it in your résumé. Very likely it will be brought up in an interview, and we'll discuss how to handle it in Chapter 8.)
3. Any honor you were awarded. Membership in scholarly organizations. If you were Phi Beta Kappa, be proud of it. Be sure it is on your résumé.
4. Brief descriptions of work history. Example: summer jobs, part-time employment, internships, co-op education programs.
5. Any languagues in which you are fluent.
6. Any skills you have, such as typing, word processing, etc. You may or may not include (in other words, it's optional) your job objective or career goal, and personal data such as military or draft status, willingness to travel or relocate, or information about your hobbies.

You must *never* insert the following in your résumé:

1. Salary expectations
2. Salaries of summer jobs
3. Name of husband or wife
4. Name and addresses of references
5. Photograph

Though there are several accepted résumé styles, the one appropriate for most recent graduates lists the facts in a historical/chronological manner.

THE HISTORICAL/CHRONOLOGICAL RESUME

As the name implies, this style of résumé presents the information in chronological succession. It is necessary, however, that the presentation be in *reverse* chronological order, starting with your present educational experience and moving backwards, listing your most recent summer experiences first.

Dates are always included. They can be displayed in a vertical column set apart from the other information or included as an integral part of each paragraph of your history. Generally the first is preferred, as most employers like to be able to determine at a glance the dates involved.

If you decide to include a job objective, it should be placed at the very beginning, after your name and address but before the descriptions of your education and work history.

Following are typical category headings and alternatives found in a college graduate's résumé.

Job Objective	Course Work
Career Objective	Course Studies
Career Goal	Representative Course Work
	Academic Concentration
Education	
Academic Experience	Honors
	Awards
Employment	Academic Achievements
Work Experience	
Work History	Special Skills
Career Experience	Additional Skills
Field Experience	Relevant Skills
	Interests
Activities	
Extracurricular	References on Request
Activities	References Available Upon Request
Campus Activities	References Furnished Upon Request

JOB OBJECTIVE OR CAREER GOAL

Deciding to use a job objective or career goal (the two mean very much the same thing) will depend on whether its use will actually increase the power of your résumé.

Remember, the use of the career goal is up to you—it's completely optional. If you do decide to use it, it should be brief—no more than two sentences. In one or two lines it should be a statement that briefly summarizes your goals and is justified by your education.

Avoid stating an objective that is too limiting. One graduate we encountered wanted a job in children's book publishing. She would, however, have been very happy to accept *any* job in publishing, whether it be trade books, textbooks, magazines, or trade journals. She sent her résumé to every publisher listed in the Yellow Pages but, unfortunately, she didn't get any bites. It is quite obvious that if a textbook publisher received her résumé and had an opening, the publisher would *not* have considered her because she specified a job in children's book publishing. Obviously her career objective was too specific. A more appropriate goal would have been "To secure an entry-level position in publishing." She might have been wiser not to include any job objective.

Be careful to avoid the use of clichés—"A challenging job where I can meet people," "A position that is both responsible and creative." Such career goals don't really say anything, and your résumé will be more professional without such a statement.

If you can transfer your education, talents or skills into a position or specific job title, that makes for an ideal job objective. For example:

Chemist
Laboratory Assistant
Staff Accountant
Salesperson Trainee
Gal/Guy Friday

Another approach is to use a field as the job objective. For example:

An entry-level position in any area of advertising
Growth spot in a major corporation

Your career goal doesn't have to be limited to either a job title or a field. It may simply be a statement of where or in which direction you hope to be going. Don't include the pronoun "I" or "me." Be sure the goal is brief, assertive, and to the point. For example:

To utilize mathematics background in the computer industry
A sales position that might ultimately lead to a career in marketing
An entry-level position in journalism

If you plan to use your résumé in a mass mailing and also to use it to respond to a large number of classified advertisements, it may be a good idea to omit the career goal and include it in the cover letter. This allows you to target your goal to the specific situation.

EDUCATIONAL HISTORY

As a recent college graduate, the most valuable asset you have to sell is your education. Therefore it is placed at the very beginning of your résumé unless you have decided to state a career goal or job objective, in which case your educational history should immediately follow that statement. If you are not including a job objective, your educational history should be placed directly under your name, address, and phone number.

Your education should be arranged in reverse chronological order. Begin with your most advanced or recent degree and work backwards until you reach your bachelor's degree. Obviously if you don't have an advanced degree, start with your bachelor's degree. It is not necessary for a college graduate to list a high school unless it was a very prestigious preparatory school and naming it might enhance the résumé.

Be sure to include the name and address (just the city; street address is not necessary) of your college or university, the date of graduation, and the degree you received. You should include your major and minor, as well as any honors that were earned. For example, here is how one individual listed undergraduate through graduate education:

> 1992 Columbia University
> New York, NY
> Ph.D. Political Science
>
> 1990 College of William and Mary
> Williamsburg, VA
> M.S., International Affairs
>
> 1989 University of Chicago
> Chicago, IL
> B.A. Phi Beta Kappa, 3.9 average
> Business Administration/Economics

Keep these tips in mind:

1. It is acceptable to abbreviate the title of your degree; that is, B.S. instead of Bachelor of Science.
2. List all honors, including langugages, scholarships, and awards.
3. You can indicate your major and minor by using the words "Major" (followed by subject) and "Minor" (followed by subject), or simply use a slash. For example, "Major: Chemistry; minor: Biology" or simply "Chemistry/Biology."
4. If you attended more than one college or university, be sure to list all of them, again in reverse chronological order. Don't forget to include dates but do omit any explanation of why you changed. This can be discussed in the interview. For example:
   1990–1992 University of Colorado, Denver, CO, B.A.
   1988–1990 New York University, New York, NY

WORK HISTORY

Even though your work history probably consists of summer and temporary jobs, it will add significant power to your résumé.

Your experience will contribute to the feeling of your being a mature, functioning adult or will—as one of our favorite clients used to say—let people know you are "office broken." Though you're looking for an entry-level position, you're not an "absolute beginner."

If you have worked on a job that relates to the career you desire, that would be ideal, but it's unlikely. Students are expected to take any kind of job they can get, and the fact that you could take a boring job and stick with it for a summer says a lot about your character and will be an asset on your résumé.

Your work background should immediately follow your educational history. Though you probably had only summer or temporary jobs, each should be listed separately. Each entry should include the name and address of the employer, the dates involved, the job title, and a brief description of your responsibilities. Keep the description succinct, but include all basic activities of each particular job. Use implied pronouns; clear, simple language; and active verbs. Don't write in the third person (it is stylistically objectionable) and don't use "I" ("I" is redundant—the person reading the résumé knows you are the subject of your own résumé). For example, don't write "He was responsible for bookkeeping," or "I was responsible for bookkeeping," but rather, "Was responsible for bookkeeping."

If you worked while in college, that should be the first job listed, and the others should follow in reverse chronological order.

If you worked through a temporary agency and were sent to several different companies, give the name and address of the temporary service, the dates you were employed, your job title, and the names of the companies you were assigned to. For example:

Part Time
1988–1991

Library Assistant
Low Library, Columbia University,
New York, NY
Catalogued books, maintained library files and revised when necessary. Handled routine requests for materials, slides, and films. Ordered books, pamphlets and magazines as needed to keep library collection up to date.

Summer:
1990, 1991, 1992

Gal/Guy Friday
Career Blazers Temporary Personnel, Inc.,
New York, NY
Was responsible for data entry on a PC and editing correspondence, manuscripts, reports, and press releases. Functioned as receptionist, set up appointments, and assumed general office duties.

The following is a list of the many action verbs you might want to use:

achieve	emphasize	invent	repair
adjust	encourage	inventory	replace
aid	enforce	investigate	research
analyze	engineer	lead	resolve
answer	establish	learn	return
arrange	estimate	liaise	review
assemble	evaluate	list	revise
assist	examine	maintain	reward
attain	execute	manipulate	satisfy
attend	expand	market	schedule
author	expedite	master	screen
benefit	facilitate	modify	select
better	familiarize	monitor	ship
budget	finish	motivate	show
calculate	forecast	move	situate
change	form	negotiate	solve
compile	formulate	operate	sort
compute	function as	order	sponsor
conceive	gain	organize	staff
conduct	gather	orient	stage
construct	govern	originate	stipulate
consult	guide	package	straighten
contribute	handle	participate	study
control	help	perform	submit
coordinate	hire	prepare	supervise
create	identity	present	supply
counsel	illustrate	process	systematize
decrease	improve	profit	train
delegate	increase	promote	transfer
deliver	inform	propose	translate
demonstrate	initiate	provide	transmit
designate	input	publish	travel
determine	inspect	purchase	troubleshoot
develop	inspire	receive	turn around
direct	instruct	recommend	utilize
display	institute	reduce	verify
distribute	interact	refer	volunteer
document	interface	refine	word process
earn	interpret	relate	
edit	interview	reorganize	

Remember that it is not necessary to use full sentences. Snappier simple phrases will be more effective.

OTHER DETAILS

Extracurricular activities can be very important. Include a description of yours; it not only paints a more rounded portrait of you, but also indicates talents and abilities not reflected in your course of study.

Membership in the college debating society implies an articulate, poised personality. A class officer will be seen as an extroverted individual with a great deal of leadership potential. Being active in sports, such as football, basketball, or tennis, indicates an individual who functions well on a team. If you have aspirations in communications, having worked on any college publications will give you an advantage.

These activities should be listed simply with no further explanation.
Editor of college yearbook
Photographer for college newspaper
Member of college debating society
President of chess club

PERSONAL INFORMATION

There was a time, before the civil rights movement, when every résumé was expected to include height, weight, age, sex, and marital status. This is no longer true. There is no reason to include such information. The information is not pertinent, nor will it strengthen your résumé.

If you are free to travel or to relocate, mention that in your résumé. Such information is solid, and would be very useful to a person screening résumés for a position out of town or requiring travel.

If you have traveled extensively, that might be of interest to certain employers and it should be noted in your résumé. The fact that your résumé shows you have been to the Far East may be the very thing that sparks the necessary interest in you to warrant an interview. Though we recommend that you include extensive travel in your résumé, we also want to remind you to keep it brief—no more than a sentence or two.

SKILLS

College graduates often make the mistake of not listing job skills they have acquired. They think holding a degree makes it unnecessary to mention that they might be excellent at typing, word processing, desktop publishing, special computer applications, copy editing, typesetting, bookkeeping, or any one of the many office machines. They are selling themselves short. Any skill increases one's marketability. If you have them, flaunt them! We had the experience of sending résumés of three college grads to a prestigious international foundation that was looking for a library/stock research assistant. Though the job specifications did not require keyboarding, the client chose to interview and hire the one person whose résumé indicated that he knew how to use a spreadsheet package on a personal computer. Their feeling was, it's always a good idea to have someone who might be able to pitch in, if necessary. The other candidates were computer literate too, but because it didn't show up on their résumés, they simply lost out.

Any knowledge of foreign languages should be noted in this section. Be sure to distinguish whether you are fluent in the language or have just a reading knowledge of it.

REFERENCES

At the very end of your résumé, state "References available upon request." Why? Simply to let your reader know where your résumé ends. Without this phrase a prospective employer may think that a page is missing.

The names of your references should never be included in your résumé. Not only is it unprofessional, but it can cause unnecessary bother to those persons listed. You should only give permission to call your references when an employer has indicated that he or she is really interested in employing you.

Always, of course, get permission from all the people you list as references before giving out their names. Try to choose people who can be reached quickly, preferably by phone rather than by mail. If you are giving the business phone of a reference, be certain that he or she is still employed by that company. If you give a woman as a reference, make sure you know whether she uses her maiden or married name.

Likewise, if your name has changed through marriage or any other reason, be sure that your references know you by your new name. It is a good idea for a married woman to indicate both her married and maiden names on her résumé.

If all your references are from college and you'll be job hunting in another city, it is a good idea to ask your references to write a paragraph or two about you to be left with the university placement office. The placement office will keep these references on file and will send them on request (some charge a small fee for this service). This is efficient and helpful in minimizing the bother to those people cooperative enough to be used as a reference. If you are using this method, be sure to indicate on your résumé that your references are available through the college placement office.

Make sure each of your references has a copy of your résumé. Not only is it courteous, but it will help him to have the facts fresh in his mind.

25 RESUME RULES FOR COLLEGE GRADUATES

We've summarized the basics for résumé writing in our 25 Résumé Writing Rules for College Graduates.

1. Don't neglect to include your phone number (this is one of the most frequently omitted pieces of information)!

2. A career objective is optional. Many job seekers *prefer résumés without objectives* because they believe a stated objective can narrow their employment opportunities.

3. Recent college graduates should *always* place educational experience first.

4. Include your school name, city and state; omit the specific street address. Show your graduation date.

5. Indicate your degree name and major/minor.

6. Never include a grade point average less than 3.0 on a 4.0 index.

7. Proceed in reverse chronological order by degree: i.e., Doctorate, Master's, Bachelor's.

8. Unless you attended a prestigious prep school, do not include high school information—no one cares.

9. If you were active in campus activities, include club names and titles.

10. Go ahead and boast about honors and awards…this is the place to do it!

11. List any volunteer activities, internships, or part-time work to display leadership traits and motivation.

12. Show all work experience to indicate the ability to balance course work and earnings activity. List dates, employer's name, city and state; include job titles if possible.

13. Use action verbs (power verbs) to describe job responsibilities.

14. Write job descriptions without using I, my, myself, me, etc.

15. Use bullets (•) to set off specific duties.

16. Use vocabulary appropriate to an industry—show you know the right buzzwords.

17. Include numbers to indicate quantitative results.

18. Mention student memberships or affiliations to emphasize credibility and seriousness of studies.

19. Be sure to include a special skills category. This should note foreign language fluency, computer abilities, and use of special equipment.

20. Never include the names, titles, or phone numbers of references, but *do* include a phrase such as "References On Request." This indicates the end of your résumé to your reader.

21. Ask for his/her permission before releasing a reference's name. Be sure your reference has a copy of your résumé.

22. Pay attention to overall layout. Check for consistency of format. A résumé needs visual appeal. One page is enough for new graduates!

23. Use only a light-colored paper stock (ideally white or cream). Use matching envelopes and paper for your cover letter.

24. Do *not* include:
    - Birthdate
    - Height/weight
    - State of your health
    - Marital status
    - Photograph of yourself
    - Testimonial letters

25. Proofread your work…absolutely no typos, misspelled words or grammatical errors!

HONESTY IS THE BEST POLICY

No matter what the circumstance, the cardinal rule in writing your résumé is absolute honesty. Include *nothing* in your résumé that isn't completely true. The truth has a way of coming out and, once caught in a lie, you will have lost your credibility, which can be fatal. Such a loss cannot be corrected and will seriously damage your reputation. It puts an additional strain on you every time you interact with someone who has read your résumé. Be proud of what you have *accomplished*. You have earned your degree and have learned to accept your weaknessess as well as your strengths. You will get a job, we promise you, on your own merits and you won't always be in fear that you'll be "found out."

Before you can actually sit down and write your résumé, you must collect all the facts. The following worksheets will help you include all the necessary information and arrange it in a concise, organized manner. The worksheets are arranged in reverse chronological order; therefore, if you keep this factual information on the same form when actually writing the résumé, you will produce a résumé that will contain all the necessary information arranged correctly.

Take time to fill out the worksheets on pages 33–36 as carefully as possible. Be sure all information is correct (it's a good idea to recheck the dates) because this information will become the heart and soul of your résumé.

RESUME APPEAL

Since your résumé is the first contact between you, a whole network of people, and your prospective employer, it is imperative that it invite reading. The physical appearance of your résumé is as important as the information it contains. Logically, no matter how good the facts included in your résumé, if it is hard to read or confusing to interpret, it will end up in the wastebasket. As a result, your superior qualifications will never be read and, therefore, never be considered. Be aware that your résumé is always competing with many others, and as a result it is scanned very rapidly. Our inquiries have shown that readers rarely give a résumé more than thirty seconds of attention to decide if it merits a more detailed reading. Obviously, the more attractive it is, the better impression it will make in those few seconds. On pages 24–28 you will find some sample layouts.

SAMPLE RESUME LAYOUT—GENERAL

Name   Phone
Address
City, State, Zip Code

Career Objective _____

Name of College _____

Location of College _____

Dates_____

Major/Minor

Degree

Class Standing

Awards, Honors, Scholarships

<u>Job Title</u> — Name of Company   Summer of _____
              Location of Company
Description of duties and responsibilities.

<u>Job Title</u> — Name of Company   Summer of _____
              Location of Company
Description of duties and responsibilities.

<u>Job Title</u> — Name of Company   Summer of _____
              Location of Company
Description of duties and responsibilities.

Languages

Skills

Willing to Relocate

References (on request)

Name

Address

City, State, Zip Code

Phone

Education: Name of College, Location of College (City, State)

from _____ to _____

Degree: Major: Minor:

Experience:
from _____ to _____ Job Title
Name of Company
Location of Company

Responsibilities _____

_____

from _____ to _____ Job Title
Name of Company
Location of Company

Responsibilities _____

_____

from _____ to _____ Job Title
Name of Company
Location of Company

Responsibilities _____

_____

Honors:

Awards:

Skills:

References: Available on request

Résumé of:

Name
Address
City, State, Zip Code

Career Objective: (optional)

Educational History:

from (date)   Degree — Name of College
to   (date)   Location of College
                                              GPA (only use if 3.0 or
                                              more out of 4.0)

                                     Major/Minor

Honors/Awards ————————————————————————————————

Employment History:

from (date)
                                     Job Title Name of Company
to   (date)   Location of Company
                                     Brief description of job duties
                                     and responsibilities.

from (date)   Job Title Name of Company
to   (date)   Location of Company
                                     Brief description of job duties
                                     and responsibilities.

from (date)   Job Title Name of Company
to   (date)   Location of Company
                                     Brief description of job duties
                                     and responsibilities.

Languages: ————————————————————

Skills: ————————————————————

References: Furnished on request

Name
Address
City, State, Zip Code
Phone

Education

From (date)   Name of College
To (date)   Location of College
                                Advanced Degree   Major   Minor
                                GPA (include only if it is above
                                    3.0 out of a possible 4.0)

From (date)   Name of College
To (date)   Location of College
                                Degree
                                GPA (include only if it presents
                                    your academic record
                                    favorably)

Honors/Awards

Date received   _____

Date received   _____

Employment History (in reverse chronological order)

From (date)   Your Job Title
To (date)   Employer, Location
summer of _____   Job duties (2 to 4 lines)

From (date)   Your Job Title
To (date)   Employer, Location
Summer of _____   Job duties (2 to 4 lines)

From (date)   Your Job Title
To (date)   Employer, Location
summer of _____   Job duties (2 to 4 lines)

Extracurricular Activities

_____

_____

Language Fluency

_____

_____

Skills

_____

References
        Furnished on request

NAME   Phone
Address
City, State, Zip Code

EDUCATIONAL HISTORY

Name of College   From (date)
Location of College   To   (date)
Advanced Degree
GPA (include only if it is above 3.0 out of a possible 4.0)

Name of College   From (date)
Location of College   To   (date)
Bachelor's Degree—Major/Minor
GPA (optional)

HONORS AND AWARDS

_____   Dates Received

_____

EXTRACURRICULAR ACTIVITIES

_____

_____

EMPLOYMENT HISTORY (summer jobs)

JOB TITLE
Name of Company   From (date)
Location of Company   To   (date)
Description of duties and responsibilities—2 to 4 lines

JOB TITLE
Name of Company   From (date)
Location of Company   To   (date)
Description of duties and responsibilities

JOB TITLE
Name of Company   From (date)
Location of Company   To   (date)
Description of duties and responsibilities

LANGUAGE FLUENCY

SKILLS

REFERENCES
Available on Request

WHAT EMPLOYERS LOOK FOR...

For many years our company has worked with the nation's most prominent corporations and organizations. As part of our research for this book, we asked some of these clients what they look for in an entry-level résumé. Here's what they said...

- Name of school—particularly if it has a prestigious academic reputation
- Appropriateness of major or minor to our job opening
- An impressive GPA
- Honors, awards, or scholarships—they display an individual's performance abilities
- Percentage of education self-financed by the candidate—it demonstrates a work ethic and initiative
- Work experience—"real world" vs. "academic." We look for good interpersonal skills, degree of responsibility, and hands-on relevance.
- Activities—participation in clubs, sports, volunteer work, and student organizations. They show involvement, dedication, energy, and sense of self.
- Special skills—we want to see things like computer proficiency, foreign language fluency and/or special certifications.

COMPUTERS AND THE COLLEGE GRADUATE

Most grads reading this book will undoubtedly have some experience using a computer. If you don't, you should—because it is one of the most in-demand skills for the current job market.

This is the age of the automated office; everyone from clerks to company presidents has a computer workstation situated near at hand. Typically, when we at Career Blazers ask a new college graduate how fast he can type or what software applications she knows, the response is, "I didn't go to college to type!" Well, of course you didn't. But the modern office has minimized the use of traditional secretaries and therefore many more job titles require keyboard literacy. For example, financial firms want people with spreadsheet or data base management, publishing houses and ad agencies expect their new hires to have word processing or desktop publishing skills, and so on down the line of all industries.

Our advice to those job seekers who are reluctant to take a software or typing test is that you are putting yourself at a tremendous disadvantage. If you know how to use a computer, say so! Be sure your résumé includes the hardware and software you are familiar with; if you happen to be a fast typist (40 + words per minute), it won't hurt your employment chances to include your speed. You'll notice that many of the model résumés in this book indicate some degree of computer fluency. Don't cut yourself out of the competition by omitting such a critical skill. (It may interest you to know that all the sample résumés produced in this book were originally created using desktop publishing or word processing software and were printed by a laser printer.)

Without a doubt, computer savvy is an asset in the job hunt. Your resumé should be professionally word processed or desktop published. It must appear clear and attractive, and look as though you are accustomed to turning out professional, accurate documents. Your cover letter should have the same general appearance; they should be a matched pair. Don't spend money on having a resume professionally produced or typeset and then spoil the effect with a handwritten cover letter. Business correspondence is never handwritten.

The hottest computer skills to include on a resume are:

- Word Processing
- Electronic Spreadsheet
- Data Base Management
- Desktop Publishing
- Programming
- System Design/Installation and Troubleshooting
- Data Entry

Again, on your resume, list the names of the software applications you can use. If you are not fully versed in a package, but know it slightly, indicate this with the phrase "familiarity with..." In a cover letter you might take your computer know-how one step further. Here's an example:

I am fully fluent in Microsoft Word on the Mac. I know advanced functions such as mail merge and outlining. I have had some exposure to PageMaker, although I am not as well versed in this package as I am in Word. I'm very eager to upgrade my skills or cross-train to other computer applications, and I look forward to expanding my software expertise.

Employers don't want to hire individuals who are computer-phobic, so indicating that you are computer-friendly is a smart strategy.

More Than a Job Skill

Now let's examine other aspects of computers in your job search. In addition to making you a more marketable candidate, computers can help you in other ways. How?

Many job openings are listed in computer data banks and "bulletin boards," which can be accessed on a computer screen via a modem. If you do not personally own a modem, investigate what your community or university library has to offer in this area. A large majority are on nationwide networks, and you can access job opening information by executing a few simple key commands. This is also a great way to gain information on a company, since many annual reports and other corporate statistics are now on line and available at the touch of your fingertips.

There are also several resumé service companies, which will put your resumé into their data banks; from there it goes out to employers nationwide who subscribe to this source as a recruitment tool. The hiring company scrolls through resumé after resumé on a computer screen in their own office. When someone's resumé interests them, they contact the service or the individual for a personal interview. Be sure to shop these services wisely so that you know your résumé is really getting into the hands of firms looking to hire, and that these job openings are compatible with your own qualifications.

Finally, there are also several software programs designed specifically for the job seeker. These programs will create a résumé, cover letter, and follow-up correspondence for you. They will also help you manage your mailing list and keep your job search organized. A note of caution, however: while these packages can be very helpful, they are frequently misused. Too often job seekers rely on the standard résumé formats and prewritten cover letters found within each software application. This can be a big mistake, since your résumé loses its unique look and your own ideas or words may not fit into their predetermined designs. Unfortunately, when you fail to customize a résumé or cover letter it generally sounds like a form letter, and generic correspondence does not impress employers. Although writing your own résumé takes time and energy, it is still the best solution and the smartest way to gain an interview.

4

DRAFTING YOUR OWN RESUME

Note that these drafts are to be considered solely as models. You may wish to vary your own résumé. We've included two worksheets, one for practice and one for your final version.

When you have filled out the worksheets, you will be well on your way to writing your résumé. The information included in the worksheets comprises the very "guts" of your résumé. For that reason you must thoroughly check what you have written to make absolutely sure everything is correct.

1. Look at the dates. Are they correct?
2. *Reread* your résumé worksheets. Is there any important information missing?
3. Examine the worksheets. Have you included any information that is *not* necessary? (Such as name of husband or wife; list of all the courses you took; name of grammar school; your salary minimum, or salaries of past jobs.)
4. Reread each of your "Job Duties." Are they as clear and as strong as possible? Have you used as many action verbs as you could? Have you *excluded* all pronouns?
5. If you listed any scholarships, will the average reader understand the nature of the scholarship?
6. Reread your worksheets *again* to make sure there are no words spelled incorrectly. Ask at least two people to proofread your worksheets, concentrating on the spelling. Use your dictionary!

Worksheet for Entry-level College Graduate

I. Name

_____

(If married woman, include married and maiden name)

Address: _____

_____

(Be sure to give home, not college, address. Give number and street, city, state, and zip code)

Phone (home): _____

(Be sure to give area code)

Phone (other): _____

It is a smart idea to purchase a telephone answering machine if you don't already own one. Record a message that sounds professional and pleasant so that potential interviewers will have a good impression of you. Avoid music, silliness, and being too glib. An employer calling to arrange an interview will favor a business-like manner over clever rhetoric.

II. Job Objective or Career Goal

Remember, the Job Objective is optional. If you decide to use it, be brief and take care that your stated objective _does not_ limit your opportunities nor is so vague as to be meaningless.

_____

_____

III. Educational Background

Begin with your most advanced degree and, in REVERSE CHRONOLOGI-CAL ORDER, list all degrees and certificates stopping with your bachelor's degree. Be sure to list the college name and location (just city and state) along with dates of attendance.

Dates: Name of University or College:

_____ _____   _____

(From)   (To)   (or the date degree received)

                   Location of School:

                   _____

                   Degree (or Credits) Earned:

                   _____

                   Major: Minor:

                   _____   _____

                   (If Ph.D., title of your dissertation instead of minor)

Dates: Name of School:

_____ _____   _____

(From)   (To)   (or the date degree received)

                   Location of School:

                   _____

Degree (or Credits) Earned:

_____

Major: _____   Minor: _____

Dates: _____   Name of School:

_____ _____   _____
(From)   (To)   (or the date degree received)
                   Location of School:

                   _____

                   Degree (or Credits) Earned:

                   _____

                   Major: _____   Minor: _____

If you changed colleges, be sure to list both.

Scholarships, honors, awards including dates:

Scholarships:

_____

Awards:

_____

Honors:

_____

Class Standing or Grade Average (list only if noteworthy):

_____

IV. Employment History (summer or part-time jobs)
Your employment history should be listed in reverse chronological order, starting with your most recent job. If you worked part-time while in college as well as during summers, list the job you held while in college first.

Dates: _____   Name of Company:

_____ _____   _____
From   To   Location of Company (City and State):
mo/yr   mo/yr
                   _____

                   Job Title:

                   _____

                   Description of Responsibilities (remember,
                   keep it brief; use action verbs):

                   _____

                   _____

                   _____

                   _____

Dates: _____   Name of Company:

_____ _____   _____
From   To   Location of Company (City and State):
mo/yr   mo/yr
                   _____

Job Title:

_____

Description of Responsibilities (remember,
keep it brief; use action verbs):

_____

_____

_____

_____

Dates: Name of Company:

____ ____   _____

From   To   Location of Company (City and State):
mo/yr   mo/yr   _____

                        Job Title:

                        _____

                        Description of Responsibilities (remember,
                        keep it brief; use action verbs):

                        _____

                        _____

                        _____

                        _____

Dates: Name of Company:

____ ____   _____

From   To   Location of Company (City and State):
mo/yr   mo/yr   _____

                        Job Title:

                        _____

                        Description of Responsibilities (remember,
                        keep it brief; use action verbs):

                        _____

                        _____

                        _____

                        _____

V. Extracurricular Activities: Class Officer, Membership in School Organizations:

_____

_____

_____

VI. Other Skills and Abilities:
Languages (indicate degree of fluency—reading, speaking, or writing):

_____

Computer Fluency (indicate hardware and software; include keyboarding speed if 40 wpm or above):

_____

_____

_____

VII. Special Interests or Hobbies (remember, this is optional):

_____

VIII. References:

Though the names, addresses, and phone numbers of your references should *never* be included in your résumé, it is a good idea to assemble all necessary data while you are preparing the résumé. That will help keep you organized. Try to have a minimum of three people as references.

Remember, though, we're just getting this information together; IT WILL NOT APPEAR ON YOUR RESUME.

Note: Give complete addresses—number and street, city, state and zip code. Give area codes with telephone numbers. (Give business address and telephone number instead of home information whenever possible.)

Name of Reference: _____

Position: _____

Company Affiliation: _____

Company Address: _____

_____

Business Phone and Extension: _____

Name of Reference: _____

Position: _____

Company Affiliation: _____

Company Address: _____

_____

Business Phone and Extension: _____

Name of Reference: _____

Position: _____

Company Affiliation: _____

Company Address: _____

_____

Business Phone and Extension: _____

FROM WORKSHEET TO RESUME

On pages 41–114 you will see a great number of sample résumés in addition to the sample layouts on pages 24–28. One of them, or a combination of several, may appeal to you as a format you might like to follow. Sketch out the form you decide to use and, with your completed worksheets, you are ready to start writing.

Don't be discouraged if the first few drafts are not completely satisfying. We're sure you have had the experience of rewriting term papers several times before handing them in. We again must stress that your résumé is such a vital part of your job campaign that every hour spent on it will ultimately pay off.

Keep in mind that your résumé will determine whether or not an employer will want to meet you. Certainly if you are not interviewed by a given company, you will have absolutely *no* chance of getting hired. If you think of your résumé as a passport to a good job—a document that can literally determine your future—you won't resent the time involved in making it the very best that you can.

After you have completed a résumé that meets with your satisfaction, take a break and *then* reread it the following day. Although you are not aware of it, you will have subconsciously mulled over the job. The next day you'll be much better able to pick up any mistakes and to fine-tune the résumé.

The next thing you have to consider before typing the résumé is the layout of the copy. You might choose the format from one of our samples. You might decide to combine two or more samples, or to start from scratch and create your own. Whatever layout you decide upon, make sure that the total effect is pleasing to the eye and easy to read, and that the different sections (identification information, educational history, work experiences, etc.) are clearly separated from one another.

We've received literally thousands of résumés at the agency and have come across every conceivable size, shape, and color. For just about three seconds the novel ones attract our staff's attention—and then they are quickly discarded. This includes résumés made to look like restaurant menus, newspapers with the headline "John Doe (or whoever) is Ready to Work," Valentines, brochures, invitations, summonses, subpoenas, licenses, diplomas, checks, money orders, telegrams, or mailgrams. Not only are we aware that our clients would have zero interest in these "imaginative" works, but they are simply too cumbersome to file.

Use standard 8½" × 11" paper; not only is this size easiest to handle and to file, but it is the most professional.

Choose a good-quality bond paper and use *only* one side. White is customary, but you may choose a pale color as long as it will contrast well with the type. Make sure the typeface is neat and easy to read. It should not be so large that it overwhelms the space it is in. It should be conservative and not too "arty."

Use your ground—the white space on the paper—effectively, even using your margins imaginatively. Use at least half-inch margins on all four sides. White space is soothing to the eye, and you should plan to interrupt your copy with enough white space to allow the reader to rest her or his eyes while reading your résumé.

Your typewriter or home computer, used with imagination and good taste, can be very helpful in creating an attractive résumé. You might use upper and lower case in combination with all caps, or if you have the appropriate software, mix various fonts and type sizes. Create borders; use dots, dashes, and asterisks for emphasis or separating sections. If your computer printer is of the dot matrix variety, bring your prepared disk to a word processing service bureau, where they can print out your text on a laser printer. It will make a world of difference in visual appeal.

If you are not really an excellent typist, it is a good idea to have a professional do it for you. Actually, whatever it costs is a small expense considering the ultimate return that a superior résumé can bring to you. Be absolutely sure that there are no typing or spelling errors—proofread, proofread, and then have a friend proofread. If you have used a typing or desktop publishing service, don't accept or pay for the résumés until they are throughly checked for accuracy. Certain résumés are discarded immediately even though the contents may be completely on target. Why? Simply because they are not dressed well. They look sloppy. They allow the reader to infer a negative image of its writer. Some of the mistakes that create a poor impression include:

no planned format (uneven margins, no spaces between categories, etc.) disorganized	misspelled words typographical errors sloppy grammatical errors

At one time employers expected every résumé they received to be typed individually. Fortunately, those days have passed. Although carbon copies (because of smudging and lack of clarity) are not acceptable, any other duplicating process that turns out clean, sharp copies may be used. Photocopying, offset printing and laser printing all give excellent results. Xerox copies are admissible as long as they are sharp, clean, and easy to read. It is obvious that if you are willing to spend the money on having your résumé printed, the results will be good looking as well as very professional.

As the success of your campaign may very likely hinge upon the appearance of your résumé, it is imperative that you choose a service that turns out a professional-looking product. These services are listed in the Yellow Pages under Copy and Duplicating Services, Offset Reproductions, Typing or Résumé Services, and Computer, Word Processing, or Desktop Publishing Service Bureaus.

It is important that your résumé be reproduced on good-quality paper. If you are having a typescript reproduced, be sure to insist on bond paper.

Don't skimp on the paper. The extra expense is minimal, and the effect it creates is well worth it. It doesn't pay to order a small number either, because the cost doesn't increase that much with the additional quantity printed. It is not unrealistic for a recent graduate to arm him- or herself with a hundred copies of a résumé.

USING A PROFESSIONAL RESUME WRITER

Although the intention of writing this book is to show you how to write your résumé yourself, we know there are some readers who will ultimately opt to have someone else write it for them. If you fall into this category, we urge you to be cautious in your choice.

Typically, you'll encounter two types of organizations calling themselves "Résumé Services."

The first is really a type shop or word processing service bureau. They will take a résumé you have written, convert it to type and then print it for you. Usually you will have some say in style and format. Such services usually use desktop publishing software to produce a résumé. In some instances, you may be able to bring in an already prepared diskette and simply have the service print it for you on a high-quality professional printer.

The second service not only formats your résumé but also writes it. The unfortunate thing is that often *you* are better off writing your own résumé than having someone else do it for you...unless you are sure of the service's credentials and expertise. For every good service there is an incompetent novice who just wants your money. So buyer beware! Here are some guidelines for judging the pros from the cons.

1. Check the service's credentials and length of service (call the local Better Business Bureau or Consumer Protection Agency—are there any complaints registered against them?).
2. Ask the writer's background and experience. Don't be intimidated!
3. How will the service go about creating your resume...what is the process?
4. How much will it cost you? What will you get for your money?
5. Get specifics...number of copies, paper quality, format options, printer quality, and envelopes.
6. Ask about turnaround time.
7. Insist on seeing samples of their work.
8. Will you have the opportunity to approve and proof copy before the actual printing?
9. What happens if you get home and find a typo or misspelled word? Will the service redo the résumé at no charge?
10. Any guarantee of satisfaction? Are you obligated to buy the résumé even if you hate it...will they redo it until you are satisfied?

5
SAMPLE RESUMES

The résumés reproduced here have been categorized by college major. We have attempted to offer you a broad group of academic experiences. If your exact major is not included here, there is probably something that is related.

You'll find résumés that fall into the liberal arts and sciences, business areas, and finally specialty categories. Some graduates have very limited work experiences; others have supplemented their academic credentials with strong summers, internships, and work/study programs. Examine the samples and notice how each résumé attempts to display the candidate's strengths and the relationship of his/her education to a business or industry. All of these résumés have a focus...clearly, the job seeker has thought carefully about the direction of his or her career and has done an excellent job of "packaging" him/herself for employment.

We encourage you to read *all* of the samples we have provided, even those whose majors are completely unrelated to your own background. Within any given résumé you may find some wording, a layout, or a helpful tip that can be of some value to your own work. All these samples are based on actual résumés of candidates who have contacted our employment service, Career Blazers. To protect each individual's privacy, we have changed names, dates, and locations. The samples that follow were produced on a Macintosh computer using Microsoft Word, PageMaker, and various type fonts. A laser printer was employed.

Remember...the goal of a résumé is never to get you a job; only *you* can do that. The purpose of a résumé is to get you the interview!

MICHAEL MORLEY

1753 Huntington Lane
Apple Valley, California 92307
714-555-1621

EDUCATION
VILLANOVA UNIVERSITY, Villanova, PA
Bachelor of Arts in Economics, May, 1992
Dean's List - Fall 1991, Spring 1992

EXPERIENCE
CHEMICAL BANK, Warren, PA
Summers 1990 and 1991
Teller
- Handled between $150,000 and $250,000 in transactions daily
- Relief teller for Select Banking
- Entered business account charges
- Participated in daily branch proof
- Handled night drop deposits
- Handled safety deposit boxes

FIRESTONE TIRE & RUBBER COMPANY, Garden Grove, CA
Summer 1988, January 1989, Summer 1989
General Service
- Transported cars between Avis Rent-A-Car and corporate office
- Purchased, for cash, auto parts from dealers
- Performed minor car repairs
- Took inventory of parts and tires
- Stocked parts and tires

ACTIVITIES
Junior Achievement
- Business Basics Program
- Taught sixth graders the importance of organization, production, management, and marketing.

Alpha Phi Delta National Fraternity
- Senior Send-off Chairman
- Planned event within a given budget. Worked with committee to purchase awards and food, and to find a location for the event.
- Pledge-class President

Economics Society
Special Olympics Volunteer
Villanova Crew

COMPUTER BACKGROUND
Data Structures and Algorithms I & II, MultiMate, WordPerfect, Lotus 1-2-3, Basic, Easy Stat

REFERENCES
Furnished upon request

ELLEN WOODCOCK
12 Prospect Street
Huntington, West Virginia 25701   **Telephone: 304-555-4481**

EDUCATION:

June 1992	College Of William & Mary, Williamsburg, VA
	B.A. in American Studies
	Specialty in American Cultural History
	Courses in Economics, English and Mathematics

EMPLOYMENT:

Summer '91   Williamsburg Conference & Visitors Center, Williamsburg, VA
Front Desk Clerk
Assisted Conference Office Manager in running day-to-day operations for conferences. Organized housing of conferees; maintained accurate financial and written records and compiled billing for all conference participants.

Summer '90   William Montgomery, Esq., Jamestown, VA
Law Intern
Assisted in preparing for litigation by researching related cases. Composed interrogatories and settlement statements for personal injury cases. Tabulated legal fees on completed cases.

Summer '89   The Bank of West Virginia, Huntington, WV
Cost Analyst Intern
Assisted on profitability project. Interviewed branch managers throughout West Virginia. Developed and maintained Lotus 1-2-3 spreadsheets to track branch profits.

SPECIAL SKILLS:
WordPerfect 5.0, Microsoft Word, Lotus 1-2-3, 20/20, Microsoft Excel, Harvard Graphics

LEADERSHIP:
Captain and Starting Pitcher, College of William & Mary Softball Team (captain 2 years; starting pitcher 4 years).

REFERENCES:
On request.

DOROTHY NELSON
72 Roberts Street
Tulsa, Oklahoma 74105
918-555-4434

EDUCATION:

June 1992

B.A., Anthropology Major
Minor in Sociology
Tulsa State College, Tulsa, Oklahoma

ACADEMIC HONORS:

1989, 1990, 1991, 1992

Dean's List
Graduated Magna Cum Laude

WORK HISTORY:

September 1990
to December 1991

Research Assistant
Museum of Natural History
Tulsa State College, Tulsa, Oklahoma
Served as Secretary to the Director of Museum.
Duties included:
- Word processing (WordPerfect 5.1)
- General office work
- Meeting and travel arrangements
- Computer data entry
- Inventory of museum displays
- Follow-up on new exhibits

Summer 1990

Clerk
Honeywell Oil Company, Tulsa, Oklahoma
General typing, word processing and reception.

Summer 1989

Tutor
Tulsa State College, Tulsa, Oklahoma
Tutored 25 students in all freshman subjects.

EXTRACURRICULAR ACTIVITIES:

1990, 1991, 1992

President, Student Chapter
American Anthropology Society.

REFERENCES:

Available on request.

JOSEPH SCARABELLI
12 Evergreen Place, Milltown, New Jersey 08850
908-555-9214

EDUCATION:

June 1992

New York Institute of Technology, Old Westbury, NY
Bachelor of Science Degree
Major: Architectural Technology

EMPLOYMENT:

June 1990 to Present

Cotrone Erectors Installation Corporation, Glen Cove, NY
Field Work/Supervision
Responsibilities: perform job-site inspection work; coordinate with Field Supervisor and report progress and quality of work to corporate headquarters; keep workers supplied with tools and machinery.
Assistant Field Supervisor
Job Site: Fielding Office Tower Complex, Mineola, NY
Responsibilities: work on-site in field office providing work orders to subcontractors; perform job-site inspections and notify headquarters of progress and quality of work.

October 1989 to May 1990

DePaola & Sons, Inc., Westbury, NY
Draftsman/Designer
Job Site: Dixon Quadrangle, Hicksville, NY
Responsibilities: commissioned to do working drawings for finish and detail work on this commercial property.

April 1989 to August 1989

North Shore Construction, Smithtown, NY
Draftsman/Designer
Responsibilities: commissioned to do working drawings for residential kitchen renovation and extension.

Summers 1986 & 1987

Four Brothers Construction Company, Camden, NJ
Carpenter/Laborer
Responsibilities: house framing and general construction.

ASSOCIATIONS:

American Institute of Architectural Students (A.I.A.S.)
Design Interests Group

REFERENCES:

Furnished upon request.

MARCIA PETERSON
2 Raleigh Street
Princeton, New Jersey 08540
(609) 555 - 2329

EDUCATION:

1988 - 1992

B.A., Art History
Vassar College, Poughkeepsie, NY
GPA 3.9
Graduated Summa Cum Laude

WORK EXPERIENCE:

1990 - 1992

Curator's Assistant
Vassar College, Poughkeepsie, NY
Assisted curator with various
collections. Assignments included
inventory, exhibitions, scheduling,
displays, lecture programs and shows.

1989 - 1990

Secretary
Art History Department
Vassar College, Poughkeepsie, NY
Assisted six professors in preparation of
lectures, slides, pictures, typing and
correspondence.

INTERESTS:

Painting, Ceramics, Music and Swimming

SPECIAL SKILLS:

Proficient on both the IBM PC and
Macintosh computers. Fluent in Microsoft
Word, PageMaker, Aldus Freehand and Excel.

REFERENCES:

On request.

Donna Sanders
16 Frawley Road
Aberdeen, Maryland 21001
301-555-1669

Education:

Towson State University, Towson, MD   1992
B.S. in Behavioral Science, Minor in Biology
Dean's List 1991 and 1992
Awarded the Crandall Medallion by Towson State Family
Service League.

Experience:

Eating Disorders Clinic, Towson, MD   1/92 - 8/92
Intern/Assistant Behavioral Counselor
Conducted behavior modification classes for clients
participating in eating disorders program. Worked with
bulimic patients. Provided counseling on an individual
basis; enlisted nutritional support from program
dietician.

Covenant House, Towson, MD   9/90 -10/91
Resident Advisor
Provided counseling and support services for 14- to 16-year-olds
living under independent conditions. Responsibilities included
preparing assessments and reviewing the results with the
Director of Operations. Involved with Intake Unit, which screened
applicants for admission into the program.

White Forest Children's Services   8/89 - 8/90
Peer Counselor
Responsibilities included providing crisis runaway intervention
counseling with youth and/or family. Acted as liaison with outside agencies on individual cases and handled runaway hotline.

References:

Furnished upon request.

BRADLEY GRUBER
40 Putnam Avenue
Tucson, Arizona 85721   *Phone: 602-555-9002*

EDUCATION:

B.S.   Arizona State University, Tempe, AZ   May 1993
Biology Major, Business Minor

EMPLOYMENT:

Mount Wendell Hospital, Tempe, AZ   1990 - 1993
Orderly
Responsible for assisting with patients in the
Intensive Care Unit and Pediatric Ward.

Powell Private Ambulance Service,   1988 - 1990
Tempe, AZ
Driver and Attendant
Coordinated daily schedules, dispatched
vehicles and handled busy switchboard.

CERTIFICATIONS:

Emergency Medical Technician
Water Safety Instructor

ACTIVITIES:

Arizona State Diving Team   1989 - 1990
Day Student Legislator

REFERENCES:

Available from the Arizona State University Placement Office,
Woodrow Hall, Tempe, AZ
602-555-3500.

KEITH J. BOYD
2267 Peach Pit Road
Miami, Florida 33152
305-555-5490

Education:

Jacksonville University, Jacksonville, Florida
B.A. in Broadcast Communications, Minor in Photography
April 1992   Graduated with Honors – 3.6 GPA.

Experience:

Freelance Editor, COURT TV, Jacksonville, Florida
Responsible for editing trial footage, pre- and post-trial interviews.
January 1992 to April 1992

Cameraman/Videographer/Production Assistant
WJCT Cable -TV, Jacksonville, Florida
Responsible for shooting news footage, interviews, press conferences,
council meetings, hearings, sports remotes and studio shows.
Received and recorded feeds, wrote scripts, edited highlights for week-
day 6 p.m. and 11 p.m. news, created sports music videos.
August 1990 to December 1991

Disc Jockey, WFIN Student Radio, Jacksonsville, Florida
Produced weekly two-hour lunch feature radio show.
October 1989 to January 1990

Qualifications:

Excellent interpersonal and verbal communication skills.
Highly developed skills on SONY editing machines: SONY 900, 901,
910, Grassvalley 110, and the Abekas 801, 802 systems.
Proficiency on Macintosh and IBM personal computers.
Strong leadership and team management skills.

Organizations :

Jacksonville University's Varsity Soccer Team (1989-1992)
Earned 50% of college tuition through Soccer Scholarship.
Participated in Loyola-Budweiser Soccer Tournament (1991)
Speaker for "Say No to Drugs" Program for Jacksonville middle schools.

References:

Available on request.

Alyssa Kramer
758 Vanderbilt Parkway
New Bern, North Carolina 28560
919-555-2057

Education:

May 1992	University of North Carolina at Chapel Hill, Chapel Hill, NC B.A. in Business Administration Major: International Business Minor: Italian GPA 3.46 Dean's List
1990	American University of Rome, Rome, Italy Studies in International Business and Advanced Italian language and culture. Dante Alighieri Institute, Florence, Italy Studies in Italian grammar and culture.

Internship:

5/89 - 8/89	Phillip Morris USA, New York, NY Summer intern for Media Coordinator Evaluated new publications; compiled data for magazine demographics; evaluated ad positioning and reproduction quality. Utilized IBM PC using WordPerfect 5.0 and Lotus. Summarized competitive product analyses for Black and Hispanic markets.

Part-time Work Experience:

12/91 to Present	Community Counseling Service, Cranston, NC Administrative Assistant/Finance Department Assist with General Ledger, Accounts Payable and Cash Disbursements for annual audit. Perform analysis of AP journal. Help prepare financial statements.
5/87 to 8/88	Chapel Hill Wellness House, Chapel Hill, NC Clerical worker performing general administrative support.

Skills: Fluent in Italian   IBM PC: WordPerfect and Lotus

Travel: Italy, France, Spain and Portugal

References: Available upon request.

DONALD McOWEN
846 Wendover Road
Waukegan, Illinois 60085
312-555-6879

EDUCATION:

1992   Northwestern University
                        Evanston, Illinois
                        B.S., Chemistry; Math Minor
                        Overall G.P.A. 3.6
                        Dean's List; Presidential Scholarship;
                        Phi Beta Kappa
                        President of Chess Club

REPRESENTATIVE
COURSE WORK: Chemistry, Analytical Chemistry, Organic
                Chemistry, Physical Chemistry, Thermo-
                dynamics, Algebra, Calculus, Differential
                Equations, Statistics, various courses in
                Russian, English, Philosophy and
                Psychology.

WORK EXPERIENCE:

Summers   Trudy, Brown & Sons Insurance
1990 & 1991   Chicago, Illinois
                 Functioned as assistant to three adjustors
                 in bodily injury division: managed cor-
                 respondence; sent out forms; ordered sup-
                 plies; coordinated police reports & motor
                 vehicle reports; set up physical exams.

Summer 1989   Chestnut Hill Country Club
                 Chicago, Illinois
                 Waiter

REFERENCES: Available on request.

MARSHA GLICK
14 Livingston Avenue
Yonkers, New York 10705   **914-555-2825**

EDUCATION: Skidmore College, Saratoga Springs, NY
               September 1989 to May 1992
               B.A. degree in Communications
               Graduated with G.P.A. of 3.50

WRITING: Co-authored The Flavor of Spring, collected stories of nursing
               home residents with photographs by the author, Halcyon
               Press, Skidmore College.

               Wrote news and feature stories for the Skidmore College
               Journal.

               Published feature articles in Penguin magazine.

EDITING: Served as *Editor-in-Chief* of 1992 Skidmore College year-
               book. Planned organization and design of book. Coor-
               dinated work of five editors, approved and edited all photos
               and copy, worked with staff at all stages of production.

               Served as *Editor-in-Chief* of Yonkers H.S. Broadcaster.

LAYOUT/DESIGN: Planned design scheme of 1992 college yearbook.
               Worked with layout editor on production of all layouts.

               Designed brochures for church youth conference.

               Earned 15 college credit hours in Art.

PHOTOGRAPHY: Shot, developed and printed pictures for college yearbook.

               Published pictures in Skidmore College Journal.

               Earned 9 college credit hours in Photojournalism.

EMPLOYMENT: Wrote news releases and did paste-up of brochures and
               pamphlets as *Assistant for Information Services*,
               Skidmore College (June-August 1991).

               Gathered class materials, administered and graded tests
               as *Teaching Assistant* to professor of Philosophy,
               Skidmore College (September 1990 - June 1991).

REFERENCES & PORTFOLIO:
               Furnished upon request.

Kathryn Allan

100 Stonehaven Drive
Boston, Massachusetts 02105
(617) 555-8432

CAREER OBJECTIVE: Entry-level position in the field of television production.

EDUCATION:

Boston University, Boston, Massachusetts
1992   B.A.   Major: Communication Arts
                 Minor: English

BROADCASTING EXPERIENCE:

BTV, Boston University Television, Boston, MA
May 1991 - August 1992

Producer
Produced *Upbeat*, weekly musical series for BTV.

Associate Director
- *Who Me?*, dramatic special for BTV
- *Ponder This*, information series for BTV

Traffic & Continuity Manager
Logged commercials in individual productions and weekly programming tapes; supervised the production of all commercials and public service announcements; reviewed all advertising copy.

Sales Representative
Sold air time to local businesses using rate card and contracts.

At various times filled in as needed in the following positions for BTV: Technical Director, Audio Engineer, Electronic Graphics, Stage Manager, Cameraman, and Videotape Editor.

EMPLOYMENT:

Financed 50% of college tuition and expenses.

Summers 1989, 1990 and 1991
Marblehead Yacht Club, Marblehead, MA
Sailing instructor for adults, teens and children. Led group sessions and one-on-one instruction for beginner and intermediate-level sailors.

May 1988 - April 1991 (part-time while in school)
Filene's, Boston, MA
Retail Sales, Fine Jewelry Department

HONORS & MEMBERSHIPS:

Dean's List 1989, 1990, 1991, 1992
Outstanding Senior Award, 1992 awarded by BTV
Women in Communications, student chapter, Boston University

REFERENCES & PORTFOLIO:

Available on request.

GLORIA SOMMER
1744 Straight Arrow Lane
Caribou, Maine 04736
207-555-1257

RELATED EXPERIENCE:
PREMIERE RADIO NETWORKS, New York, NY   Summers 1991, 1990
Sales Assistant
-Reported daily to V.P. Eastern Sales
-Acted as a liaison between client and sales reps
-Extensive market research using Marketron and MRI
-Initiated and implemented a sales analysis program for the New York office
-Updated sales records, which included post analysis and contracts
-Responsible for the coordination and trafficking of promotional material and media kits
-Compiled information and prepared presentations
-Duties included training other assistants and overseeing their work in progress

INTERNSHIPS:
NEWSWEEK MAGAZINE, New York, NY   Fall/Winter 1990
Communications/Publicity Assistant
-Wrote nomination letters for 1991 magazine awards
-Organized data for media reports
-Distributed press clips for external and internal communication

AMERICAN CANCER SOCIETY, New York, NY   Fall 1989
Communications Intern
-Wrote press releases regarding numerous special events, e.g., *The Great American
 Smokeout*
-Presented public relations materials at various health fairs
-Coordinated mass mailing list for annual gala

SKILL REVIEW:
•Effective communicator, both verbally and in written form; comfortable making
 presentations before groups
•Strong sales experience
•Strong knowledge of WordPerfect 5.0/5.1, PFS Write, Lotus 1-2-3, Harvard Graphics,
 Marketron, MRI and Lexis/Nexis

EDUCATIONAL BACKGROUND:
B.A., Communication Arts/Public Relations   May 1992
Colby College, Waterville, Maine

REFERENCES:
Furnished upon request

SAMUEL DAHLBERG
54 Rumford Road
Monticello, Arkansas 71655
501-842-6275

EDUCATION:

New Hampshire College, Manchester, New Hampshire   January 1993
>   Major: Computer Information Systems
>   Minor: Business Administration
>   *Completed four-year academic program in three years.*

ACCOMPLISHMENTS:

Systems Analysis, Design & Development
- Performed full life cycle system analysis of a sample Hospital MIS using Yourdon's system development methodology. As a case study, designed and developed it using COBOL and ISAM files, then enhanced to a database-oriented system using SQL.

Simulation & Modeling
- Developed a GPSS-based simulation model requiring use of probabilistic theories and cost benefit analyses.

Artificial Intelligence
- Utilizing Turbo PROLOG, designed a knowledge-based expert system to evaluate and qualify international applicants for admission to New Hampshire College.

Marketing Management
- Developed a first-level marketing plan outlining the market situation, opportunity and growth potential for a new restaurant in Manchester/Nashua, NH area.

SKILLS:

Hardware:	IBM PC, PS/2 and compatibles, VAX, IBM 4341
Operating Systems:	MS/DOS, VAX/VMS, IBM/VM
Languages:	GPSS, Turbo PROLOG, SQL, COBOL, C
Software Tools:	VP EXPERT, dBASE III Plus, Lotus 1-2-3, NEWS, Flow Charting, Quattro, BriefCASE, WordStar, WordPerfect, PrintMaster, Harvard Graphics

ACTIVITIES:

- **Resident Assistant, New Hampshire College**   1991 to 1992
Responsible for planning and conducting various social, cultural and educational programs in assigned residence location; provided 24-hour supervision for 36 students, and assistance in confronting various academic and personal issues.

REFERENCES:

>   Furnished upon request.

JANICE MAYBERRY

1921 East 16th Street
Rock Island, Florida 33314
813-555-2146

EDUCATION: FLORIDA STATE UNIVERSITY
Tallahassee, Florida
Degree: Bachelor of Arts, Computer Science, May 1992

SKILLS: COMPUTEERS: IBM 286, 486, PS-2 and compatibles
SOFTWARE: WordPerfect, Symphony, Volkswriter, WordStar, DOS, PC Tools, Lotus 1-2-3/Quattro Pro, Notebook, Deluxe Paint, DrawPerfect, PC Paintbrush, Communications Software, dBASE III+, Light Microsoft Windows, Word and Paradox
OTHER: Installation of software/hardware and light programming of computers

EMPLOYMENT: 2/92-4/92
<u>NORDIC CAPITAL GROUP, INC.</u>
New York, New York
Administrative Assistant
- Managed PC network for administrative staff; instructed coworkers on use of specific software applications
- Coordinated and maintained calendar and employee schedules
- Arranged all travel plans for principals and vice presidents
- Composed correspondence and maintained form letters
- Maintained computers, phones, postage machine, faxes, copiers and supply inventory
- Extensive phone contact with clients

1/88-4/91
<u>FLORIDA STATE UNIVERSITY</u>
Tallahassee, Florida
Administrative Assistant to the Director, Women's Studies Program
- Maintenance of computer programs and data files
- Responsible for programming/batch files for file maintenance and system backup
- Prepared newsletter, flyers and brochures for colloquiums and events
- Composed and typed memos, letters, tests and class readers
- Maintained small library
- Trained staff in use of computer and other office duties
- Assembled new office computer (IBM PS-2) and installed programs

1987-1991
<u>CONGREGATION BETH-EL</u>
Tallahassee, Florida
Teacher
- Taught 3rd, 4th, 7th and 9th grade Religious School, Hebrew II, Hebrew III, Bar/Bat Mitzvah Class

REFERENCES:

Furnished upon request

CAITLIN GARVEY
190-75 Park Circle
Amherst, Massachusetts 01002
413-555-1392

CAREER OBJECTIVE: Entry-level opportunity with publishing company.

EDUCATION: Boston College, Chestnut Hill, Massachusetts
B.A. in Creative Writing Minor in American Literature
May 1993
Editor of *Cat's Pajamas* Literary Magazine 1992 & 1993

COMPUTER SKILLS: IBM PC and Macintosh Computers
Software: WordPerfect 5.1, Appleworks, Aldus PageMaker, dBase III+

EXPERIENCE: *Career Blazers Temporary Personnel, Boston, MA*
Administrative Assistant
January 1992 to December 1992
Sent out on a diverse group of temporary assignments lasting from one day to three weeks.
Performed clerical duties such as word processing, filing, phones, travel arrangements and special projects including newsletter layout.
Assignments included Boston Alliance for the Homeless, Global Press, and Administrative Offices of Boston Pops Orchestra.

Cobb & Horn Direct Mail Advertising, Agawam, MA
Assistant Sales Coordinator
May 1991 to August 1991
Marketed to new companies; recorded and checked on progress with new companies. Designed a new marketing technique to generate sales leads. Wrote contracts. Gained exposure to advertising copywriting and direct mail promotions. Worked with U.S. Post Office on bulk mail regulations.

Rainer Portrait Studios, Boston, MA
Telemarketing Manager
June 1989 to December 1990
Sold portraits, scheduled customer appointments, handled all aspects of customer relations, recorded daily accounts and computed weekly sales figures. Supervised and scheduled a staff of 9 to 13 part-time employees. Interviewed, hired and trained employees.

Other employment while in school included cashier, waitressing, and typing and proofing of other students' work.

REFERENCES: On request.

Gayle Stanley
148 Red Oak Path
Avon, Connecticut 06001
203-555-7711

EDUCATION:
Salve Regina College, Newport, Rhode Island   May, 1992
Bachelor of Arts in Criminal Justice/Politics
GPA of 3.41

HONORS:
Outstanding Young Women of America   Pi Sigma Alpha Honorary Society
Who's Who Among Students   Sigma Phi Sigma Honorary Society
Dean's List   Graduated with Honors

FIELD EXPERIENCE:
State of Connecticut Office of Adult Probation   1/92 - 4/92
Volunteer
   • Courtroom intake interviews and defendant processing

Rhode Island General Assembly State Government Internship   9/91 - 12/91
Rhode Island Criminal Defense Attorneys Association
   • Legislative analysis of defense issues

Concerned Students for Juvenile Justice   8/89 - 5/92
Program Creator/Volunteer Coordinator
   • Coordinated student services for juvenile residents

WORK EXPERIENCE:
Residence Hall Reception,   5/90 - 12/91
Salve Regina College, Newport, Rhode Island
       • Controlled security and registration
       • Secured integrity and safety of premises

Customer Food Services,   1/90 - 8/90
Riverfront Pub, Newport, Rhode Island
       • Responsible for hosting and servicing customers

Assistant Manager,   Summers '87, '88 & '89
Avon Sweet Shop, Avon, Connecticut
       • Supervised and trained employees

SKILLS:
Word processing with IBM DisplayWrite 3 and 4

INTERESTS:
Travel, sports, nature, poetry, foreign culture

REFERENCES:
Furnished upon request

THERESA VITULLI

21 Brite Avenue
Scarsdale, New York 10583
914-555-7336

EDUCATION:

1988 - 1992
Bachelor of Arts
University of Minnesota, Twin Cities, MN
Major in Drama   ***Minor in Dance***

1986 - 1987
Richmond College, London, England
Audition Acceptance Program affiliated with The Royal Academy of Dramatic Arts

EXPERIENCE:

1991   Teaching Assistant -- Course: Improvisation
        University of Minnesota

1989 & 1990 (Summers)
        Assistant Dance Teacher to Ms. Rita Chalice
        Cooperative Dance Association of Westchester, New York

1987   Alvin Ailey Dance Company
        Scholarship Candidate

PERSONAL:

- Appeared in and/or directed five major productions at the University
  of Minnesota
- Widely traveled in Europe
- Fluent in French and Italian
- Volunteer for Ronald McDonald House, Minneapolis, Minnesota

REFERENCES &/or AUDITIONS:

        Upon request

Jane Creasey
1248 Williams Court
Raleigh, North Carolina 27611
919-555-8704

Language Ability:
Japanese - Advanced speaking and reading

Work History:

1990 - 1991
Business Manager, Cinderella Apparel, Hirakata, Osaka, Japan
Oversaw design and manufacturing operations of independent clothing company.
Company sales increased 450% in one and a half years. Staff grew from 3 to 12.
Researched markets. Balanced accounts.

1990 - 1991
Language Instructor, PLJ Inc., Chuo-ku Osaka, Japan
Instructed engineers, research scientists, and businessmen at Sumitomo Chemical,
Ciba-Geigy Japan, Omron Electric and Tokyo Rubber. Proofread and edited
research reports and presentation material for international conferences. Lecture
in Japanese and English. Developed Business English courses for students of
various levels.

1989 - 1990
Head Instructor, KFN Inc., Kita-ku Osaka, Japan
Promoted from instructor to head instructor in three months. Managed teaching
staff of 15. Interviewed and trained new instructors. Developed course materials.
Liaison between Japanese and foreign staff.

Education:
1984 - 1992 (Interrupted academic pursuits to travel, work and live in Japan.
Goal was to gain full understanding of the language, people and culture.)
University of North Carolina, Chapel Hill
B.A. in East Asian Studies - 1987

1988 - 1989
Kansai Gaikokugo Daigaku - Hirakata, Osaka
Exchange Student - Political Science

References:
Furnished upon request

JAMES MENDEL

8 Grandview Drive
Lawrence Harbor, NJ 08879
201-555-1805

EDUCATION

THE WHARTON SCHOOL
University of Pennsylvania, Philadelphia, PA
Bachelor of Science in Economics, May 1992
Concentration in Strategic Management
GPA: 3.11

Coursework at Wharton included:

Micro and Macro Economics	Business Policy
Finance	Accounting
Statistics	Marketing
Organizational Design	Psychology
Organizational Behavior	Business Law

Entrepreneurial Decision Making - Semester-long research-oriented course focusing on the development of an actual business plan. Project included financial data collection as well as gathering marketing information.

Activities and Honors - Alpha Epsilon Pi fraternity, Scholarship Chairman; Wharton Finance Club: winner of 1989 Wharton Financial Simulation, committee member of 1990 Wharton Financial Simulations, AT&T Investment Challenge participant; intramural volleyball and football; ice skating club.

EXPERIENCE

ALBERT & GALLUP, Counselors at Law, Livingston, NJ (Summer 1990)
Legal Assistant
Aided three attorneys in tax court casework. Responsible for writing transcript summaries, preliminary case research and preparation of tax appeals.

WHARTON FINANCE DEPARTMENT, Philadelphia, PA (1989-1990)
Research Assistant
Responsible for utilizing resource material and collecting, recording and analyzing junk bond data for Wharton study on junk bond yields.

RUMSON INTERNATIONAL, INC., Wayne, NJ (Summers 1988, 1989)
Assistant Credit Manager
In charge of establishing credit ratings for accounts of major glass importer. Ordered and analyzed Dun & Bradstreet Reports. Provided customer service. Assisted with several projects concerning customer financial obligations.

PERSONAL

Knowledge of Microsoft Word, Excel and Lotus 1-2-3
Interest in stock and option investment games

REFERENCES

Furnished upon request

HOWARD FLOOD
4 Hobart Court
White Plains, NY 10601
914-555-1943

EDUCATION:

December 1992   **Pennsylvania State University**, State College, PA
Bachelor of Science Degree
Major: Economics

December 1988   **Westchester Community College,** Scarsdale, NY
Associate of Business Degree
Major: Accounting

EMPLOYMENT:

Financed 40% of college education through part-time restaurant employment.
Responsibilities included:
- Providing customer service.
- Supervising 40 employees to ensure polite and efficient service.
- Processing and administering weekly computerized payroll.
- Coordinating take-out and delivery service.
- Managing food and beer inventory.
- Working with chef on the preparation of specials.
- Accounting for all cash registers at end of shifts.
- Waiting tables and tending bar.

May - August 1992   Coco's Place, New York, NY
Floor Manager/Waiter/Bartender

May - August 1991   Istanbul Cafe, New York, NY
Assistant Manager/Waiter/Bartender

May - August 1990   MYOB Restaurant, Armonk, NY
Headwaiter

June - August 1989   O'Neal's Catch 22, Chappaqua, NY
Waiter

SPECIAL SKILLS:

IBM Personal Computer: Lotus 1-2-3, dBase III, WordPerfect
PASCAL

REFERENCES:

Available on request

RITA WYNN
6 Eustace Court
Croton-on-Hudson, New York 10520
914-555-4492

WORK EXPERIENCE:

September 1991
to December 1991:

Sweet Hollow Elementary School, Chappaqua, NY
Student Teacher, Kindergarten
--Utilized thematic approach to implement developmentally
appropriate curriculum.
--Techniques included: Writer's Workshop, Hands-on Mathematics,
Multi-Sensory Science Program.
--Adapted Madeline Hunter techniques to early childhood
curriculum.
--Coordinated and supervised parent involvement in classroom
activities.
--Planned all details for class trip to Butterfly Farm.

Summer 1991

Skytop Day Care Village, Yonkers, NY
Assistant Curriculum Coordinator
--Researched, organized and developed new thematic
curriculum appropriate for mixed-age preschoolers.

INTERNSHIPS:

September 1989
to June 1990

South Bennington Elementary School, Bennington, VT
Dance Teacher for 5- to 6-year-olds (college fieldwork)

September 1988
to June 1989

Bennington College Early Childhood Center, Bennington, VT
Teaching Intern for Grades 3 and 4.

EDUCATION:

June 1992

Bennington College, Bennington, Vermont
Bachelor of Science Degree
Major: Early Childhood Development
Minor: Psychology

REFERENCES:

On request

Roberta Steinway

289 Pleasant Lane
East Northport, NY 17731
516-555-2526

Education

Hofstra University, Hempstead, New York
Major in Electronic Journalism/Programming/Production, minor in Psychology
Date of Graduation: May 1992

Work Experience

June - August 1991 **AZTEC MEDIA ENTERPRISES**
Huntington, New York
- Producer and Director of various radio commercials
- Company liaison to all Long Island radio stations and print publications

December 1990 - **CABLEVISION OF LONG ISLAND**
January 1991 Hauppauge, New York
June - August 1990 Assistant to Director of Government Relations
- Editor and Reporter for <u>V Cable Signals,</u> the bimonthly company newsletter
- Wrote press releases concerning various subjects
- Responsible for the formation of the Cablevision/School Partnership
- Managed correspondence related to the Partnership
- Consolidated and reorganized departmental files

June - August 1989 **ALLSTAR VIDEO STORE**
June - August 1988 Bellmore, New York
Part Time: 1988 -
Present
- Assisted with start-up of overall business
- Writer, editor and distributor of customer newsletter
- Designed and managed telemarketing survey and other promotional activities

Skills & Activities

Society of Professional Journalists/Press Club of Long Island
WRHU - Radio Hofstra University News Writer
HTV - Hofstra Television Production Assistant and Camera Operator
The Chronicle - Hofstra Weekly Newspaper Special Reporter
Knowledge of Spanish
Word processing skills on the MacWrite, Wang and IBM systems

References

Furnished upon request

ARNOLD MASTERS

108 Madera Court
Roswell, Georgia 30075
404-555-9100

Objective:

Position in the Structural and/or Geotechnical field in a Design capacity

Education:

B.E. in Civil Engineering, December 1992
Georgia Institute of Technology, Atlanta, Georgia

A.A.S. in Civil Technology, May 1988
Southern Technological Institute, Marietta, Georgia
Financed 50% of college education.

Experience:

January 1990 to Present
Schoor Associates, Atlanta, Georgia
Diversified free-lance engineering services.
Responsibilities include energy surveys for implementation of energy management systems; design of high-rise and computer facilities; fire detection and prevention systems. Drafting services for private consulting firms in the mechanical, electrical and plumbing fields.

May 1988 to December 1989
Independent Contractor/Carpenter, Atlanta, Georgia
Performed carpentry work for real estate firms and commercial projects in the Atlanta area.

Honors:

Chi Epsilon, Civil Engineering Honor Society
Dean's List (ranked in top 25% of graduating class)
Member A.S.C.E.

Miscellaneous:

Speak and write Portuguese; working knowledge of Spanish
Available for travel and relocation.

References:

Furnished upon request.

WILLIAM HUNTINGTON
71 Schuyler Drive
Avon Lake, Ohio 44012
(216) 555-2587

OBJECTIVE:

To obtain an entry-level position in the Electrical Engineering field.

EDUCATION:

Boston University, Boston, MA   *1/92*
Major: Electrical Engineering
GPA 3.8/4.0   Graduated Summa Cum Laude   Dean's List every semester
Member of Tau Beta Pi, Engineering Honor Society

COURSES:

Small Computer Systems	Signals and Systems	Microprocessors
Control Systems	Logic Design	Electronics

PROJECTS:

- Designed & coded card reader using Motorola MC68HC05C4 Microcontroller.
- Designed & coded 4 computer to 2 printer interface using 8085A CPU.
- Designed & implemented ALSU for small computer system using VEM software.
- Designed and built low-power AM transmitter.

EMPLOYMENT:

Parthenon Corp., Marlborough, MA   *1/89 - 8/90*
Cooperative Work-Study Program
- Wrote programs in C & Assembly to test 15 MIP singleboard computer.
- Designed wire connections and pin assignments for IO connector/PC card.
- Performed schematic capture of Naval Communication printed circuit board on IBM XT.

Boston University, Boston, MA   *9/87 - 9/91*
Game Room Attendant
Performed minor repairs on video games; supervised student crowds; handled cash register.

SKILLS:

Software:	Pascal, Lisp, Assembler, Workview, Mentor
Hardware:	IBM 3090, Encore Multimax, IBM XT/AT, Apollo 3000
Operating Systems:	VPS, Unix 2200, MS-DOS, VMS

REFERENCES:

Furnished upon request.

JAMES L. ROTH

Campus Address:
493 Fairfield Beach Road
Fairfield, Connecticut 06430
203-555-2154

Home Address:
Sunset Park Road
Sag Harbor, New York 11936
516-555-5454

Personal Summary:
- ❏ Financed 40% of academic expenses through full- and part-time employment while in school.
- ❏ Experienced team leader with proven work ethic.
- ❏ Extensive foreign travel.
- ❏ Bilingual English/Spanish.
- ❏ Exceptional interpersonal skills.

Education:
B.A., Fairfield University, Fairfield, Connecticut   May 1993
Major: English   Minor: Business Administration
Coursework included 9 credits in Marketing & 12 credits in Communications.

Employment History:
The American Hotel, Sag Harbor, NY   Summer 1992
Provided general customer service for hotel guests: front desk/concierge; phone reservations and restaurant recommendations.

Seaview Auto Parts Corp., Bridgeport, CT   June 1990 - April 1992
Responsible for inventory control, shipping and receiving, and tax computations. Also performed service attendant duties for second shift operation in manager's absence. (Worked approximately 35 hours per week while carrying full course load.)

Fisherman's Cove, Sag Harbor, CT   Summer 1991
Fulfilled a variety of duties including hosting and waiting tables. Progressed into a junior supervisory position responsible for management of 5 busboys and handling of large sums of money.

Activities:
Manager, Fairfield University Men's Glee Club
Member of New England Yachtsman (Fairfield University Sailing Club)
Registration Committee Member
Freshman Orientation Committee Chairperson
Commencement Committee Member

References:
Furnished upon request.

Cynthia Caplune
104 Dartmouth Court
Hartford, Connecticut 06101
203-555-7724

Education:

Syracuse University, Syracuse, NY
School of Human Development
Bachelor of Science   May 1992
Major: Environmental Design (Interiors)
Minor: Architecture

Syracuse University Study Abroad
Amsterdam and Paris: Summer 1991
        Museum Studies in Dutch Art and Modern Art
Florence: Summer 1989
        Design/Conservation and Restoration Studies

Work Experience:

Smithsonian Institution, Washington, DC   August, 1990
Experimental Gallery Internship
        Built gallery model; researched artists; brainstormed ideas for entrance video to gallery
        and helped plan and review future exhibits.

Reynolds Naughton, Architect, New Haven, CT   June - August 1988
        Edited, drafted, organized blueprints for Calhoun College of Yale University.

Bennetton, New Haven, CT   June - August 1987
        Promoted product line; sales; inventory and visual merchandising.

Activities:

Student Chapter Representative, the American Society of Interior Designers	1989 - 1992
Member of Gamma Phi Beta National Sorority	1989 - 1992
Cooperative Education Advisory Board	1990 - 1991
Student Leader for Museum Studies Program (Amsterdam and Paris)	1990
Volunteer in Interior Design Resource Room	1988 - 1989
Peer Advisor	1988 - 1989
Member of Planning Committee and Exhibitor in Environmental Design Show	1989
Member of the League of Women Voters	1989

References and Portfolio:

        Furnished upon request.

LOUISE CHAMBERS
Route 9 • Brentwood, Tennessee • 37027
615-555-6533

EDUCATION

University of Iowa, Iowa City, Iowa   December 1992
B.A.   Dual Major: European History/Art History
         Minor: Photography

* Basque Consortium, San Sebastian, Spain   1990
* Studio School of the Aegean, Samos, Greece   1991

EMPLOYMENT

Craig, Higgins & Barr, Inc., Chicago, Illinois   Summer 1992
Intern/Administrative Assistant
Department of 19th Century European Painting
* Responsible for responding to telephone and written inquiries relating
  to actual and/or potential consignments for current and/or future sales.
* Catalogued consignments; researched and evaluated artists' auction
  value; established auction reserve.

City of Iowa City, Iowa   Summer 1991
City Photographer
* For press and official usage, photographically documented city-
  initiated construction from project start-up through completion.
* Planned and executed shoots; developed and printed B & W
  and 4/C material.

Department of Art, University of Iowa   1990 - 1992
Darkroom Monitor
* Managed student usage; mixed chemicals; instructed students in use of
  equipment, development and printing techniques.

SKILLS

Computer: WordPerfect, WordStar
Language: Fluent Spanish; reading knowledge of French

REFERENCES

On request

SUSAN PECK

34 Lester Street
Woodbridge, NJ 08857
908-555-3245

OBJECTIVE: To pursue a career within the fashion industry

EDUCATION: BA, August 1992
Montclair State College, Upper Montclair, NJ
Major - Fashion Studies

WORK EXPERIENCE:

(Part-time while in school)

CASUAL CORNER, Woodbridge and Monmouth, NJ, stores
Assistant Manager
1/91 - Present
- Supervise a staff of 15 sales and support people
- Accessories Manager - raised from 5% to 8% of total sales
- Responsible for all store operational procedures

LACE & TRIMMINGS, New York, NY
Sales Associate
8/89 - 1/91
- Responsible for sales and services to assigned clients
- Generated new client activity
- Coordinated with contractors for company special orders
- Handled showroom and outside sales
- Participated in trade shows

MACY'S, Monmouth, NJ
Support Position
6/89 - 8/89
- Merchandising sales floor
- Worked with Buyers on floor plans
- Performed backroom operations

RELATED COURSEWORK:

Clothing and Culture	Organizational Behavior
Color Studies	Interior Design
History of Costume	Textiles
Accounting	Intro to Marketing
Foundation of Design	Sales Concepts & Practices
Management Process	Textile & Apparel Industry

INTERESTS: Music, dancing, reading, football

REFERENCES: Furnished upon request

MARTIN E. WINSLOW

56 Bay Cove
Stonington, CT 06378
203-555-3542

EDUCATION:

FLORIDA ATLANTIC UNIVERSITY, Boca Raton, FL
MBA, emphasis in Finance, August, 1992

THE UNIVERSITY OF CONNECTICUT, Storrs, CT
BA Mathematics-Actuarial Science, August, 1989

WORK EXPERIENCE:

October 1989 to Present
WILLOW PARK COUNTRY CLUB, Pompano Beach, FL
Golf Cart / Clubhouse Attendant
Provided golf cart and bag handling/storage service to golfers and club members. Assisted in the scheduling, control and operation of several large golf tournaments. (Part-time employment to finance 100% of graduate school expenses.)

July 1987 - August 1989
ABBOTT INC. REINSURANCE INTERMEDIARIES, New York, NY
Division of Torrance Clarke
International Marine Reinsurance Accountant
Administered the prompt settlement of accounts between clients and reinsurers. Generated billings and distributed funds to clients/reinsurers with the use of a computerized accounting system. Prepared reports of uncollected balances from insolvent reinsurers.

Summer 1986
IBM CORPORATION, Danbury, CT
Vendor Payments Accountant
Investigated the receipt of goods and services for approval of payments to suppliers. Prepared weekly progress reports on the reduction of unaccounted payables. Organized records and files using Lotus 1-2-3 on an IBM PC.

ACTIVITIES:

FAU MBA Association; Sigma Phi Epsilon Fraternity: Rush Chairman 1988, Executive Committee 1988-89, Chaplain 1985; Greek Week Events Committee 1988; Math Tutor: Math Center 1986-87; various intramural sports.

REFERENCES:

Furnished upon request.

JOSHUA CARMICHAEL
53 Lincoln Path
Adrian, Michigan 49221
517-555-1249

OBJECTIVE: A customer service position in an art-related environment.

EDUCATION: Michigan State University, East Lansing, MI 1992
Bachelor of Fine Arts

WORK EXPERIENCE:

Customer Service
J.C. Penney, Lansing, MI
Summer 1992
Responsible for sales, inventory, merchandise ordering, and customer service.

Gallery Assistant
East Shore Gallery, Detroit, MI
Summer 1991
Answered phones, performed general office work, including client contact, counting inventory, and installing shows.

Field Producer
Cable News Network, Detroit, MI
Summer 1990
Investigated, developed, and produced news stories as an intern.

Executive Director
Whisper Campus Productions, East Lansing, MI
1990 - 1992 (part-time while in school)
Negotiated contracts, promoted entertainment, did fund raising, designed advertising and supervised staff.

Program Assistant
National 4-H Council, Washington, DC
Summer 1989
Organized tours; taught classes; coordinated meetings with congressmen, agencies, and program participants.

ACTIVITIES: Director of Promotions, Concert Council, Michigan State University
Chairman, Great Issues Lecture Series, Michigan State University
*Financed 100% of college expenses

REFERENCES: Furnished upon request

FREDERICK J. ARDMORE
115 Morning Glory Terrace #7D
Charlottesville, VA 22903   **804-555-6895**

EDUCATION

Bachelor of Arts, University of Virginia   May 1992
Major: Spanish   Minor: Mathematics   GPA 3.47/4.0

ACADEMIC COURSEWORK

Spanish:

> Business Spanish, Translation, Phonetics, Grammar Review, Linguistics, Sociolinguistics, Composition, Literary Analysis, Spanish Culture & Civilization

Mathematics

> Calculus I, II & III, Operations Research, Statistics, Probability, Linear Algebra, Algebra Coding, Theory of Crystals

EXTRACURRICULAR ACTIVITIES

Jefferson House, Charlottesville, VA   Booster Program Volunteer
> Acted as teacher's assistant for a local elementary school. Provided one-to-one assistance to students with special learning needs.

Charlottesville Volunteer, Reading Partner
> Provided reading and academic assistance to underprivileged children in the Charlottesville community. Utilized Spanish language skills.

University of Virginia, Black Student Alliance
> Member of Fund-raising Committee. Organized, planned and executed numerous fund-raising activities.

WORK EXPERIENCE

Tyler's Hardware, Charlottesville, VA   Summer 1988 to present
> Work 25 hours weekly while in school, full-time in summer. Maintain inventory, conduct sales, order merchandise, update database.

REFERENCES
Available upon request.

JOANNE CANDRY

5918 Sunny Drive
Las Vegas, Nevada 89106
702-555-2839

EDUCATION

University of Nevada, Las Vegas, Nevada   1992
B.A. Geography, Minor Geology
Magna Cum Laude

PROJECTS & INTERNSHIPS   1990 - 1992

- <u>District Regional Planning Commission, Las Vegas, Nevada</u>   Spring '92
  Land Use Survey via aerial photo interpretation; ground truth checking.

- <u>University of Nevada, Las Vegas, Nevada</u>   Fall '91
  Satellite image and air photo interpretation. Produced cartographic products
  via computer, photo/mechanical and manual techniques.

- <u>Las Vegas Mining Commission, Las Vegas, Nevada</u>   Spring '91
  Compiled, designed and produced a map of Nevada mineral occurrences.

- <u>Las Vegas Cultural Center, Las Vegas, Nevada</u>   Fall '90
  Identified and organized mineral specimens.

- <u>Nevada Geological Observatory, Las Vegas, Nevada</u>   Spring '90
  Served as volunteer; organized map data.

SPECIAL SKILLS

Cartography: graphic design, computer mapping, drafting, darkroom
techniques, color separation and printing, shooting and developing film.

Remote Sensing: digital image processing, statistical data analysis, manual
interpretation of satellite imagery.

Geology: Knowledge of landforms, rocks and minerals.

Computer: GeoVision, GlobalHand and WordPerfect 5.1.

EMPLOYMENT

Administrative Assistant, The Mirage Hotel, Las Vegas, NV   4/90 - 8/92

Receptionist, Library Communication System
University of Nevada, Las Vegas, NV   7/89 - 2/90

REFERENCES

Upon request.

LEONARD BRANCH
9 Newfield Road
Toledo, Ohio 43601
419-555-2278

EDUCATION:

Kent State University, Warren, OH
B.A. Government, May 1992
Additional courses in Sociology and International Development
GPA 3.5/4.0

WORK EXPERIENCE:

Summer 1992

<u>Staff Assistant, Senator Mitchell Shore, Washington, D.C.</u>
Assisted staff in areas of education, foreign relations, judiciary, press, constituent correspondence, and reelection campaign. Drafted speeches, prepared briefs, performed legislative research, and created and distributed press releases. Worked directly with various government agencies, such as the Agency for International Development. Served as the Assistant Coordinator for the Senior Citizen Internship Program.

Summer 1991 &
Summer 1990

<u>Assistant to Dept. Head, Office of Labor Relations, City of Toledo</u>
Worked with Toledo Retirement Board to review and analyze current disability-retirement cases in order to identify candidates for re-examination. Researched, designed, and produced wage assessment reports. Assisted with contract negotiations, budgetary issues, layoff policy and interdepartmental coordination. Drafted legal briefs and designed and implemented office filing system.

Spring 1989

<u>Assistant to Director of Promotion, WPNC, Norton, Ohio</u>
Responsible for station's public relations with both listeners and advertisers. Coordinated concert and special event promotions. Drafted press releases. Performed administrative duties throughout the station.

Winters 1992 &
1991

<u>Professional Ski Patroller, Heavenly Valley, Lake Tahoe, Nevada</u>
Rescued and evacuated injured skiers while providing first aid and basic life support. Taught skier safety. Responsible for crowd management and rule enforcement. Maintained heavy customer relations on a day-to-day basis.

ACTIVITIES:

Entrepreneurs Club, Kent State University	1989-1992
Entertainment Committee, Kent State University	1989-1991
Kent State Hockey Team	1988-1989
Manager, League All-Star Team: City Champions	1989

SKILLS:

Apple: Microsoft Word, MacWrite
IBM: WordPerfect, Lotus 1-2-3
Honeywell Mainframe System

REFERENCES:

On request

MAXINE SELLERS
159 West 88th Street #6B
New York, New York 10024
212-555-6377

EDUCATION:
5/92

Columbia University, New York, NY
B.A. History   Graduated Summa Cum Laude

WORK HISTORY:
1/91 to present

Heflin, Fredericks, Dobbs & Berner, New York, NY
Part-time Legal Assistant.
Type, correct and black-line legal documents.
Answer phones. Handle client billing.

5/90 to 5/92

The Family Tree, Inc., New York, NY
Founder
Started small mail-order business. Coordinated research
and production of black genealogical and historical manuscripts. Hired, trained and managed over 30 research
assistants. Produced and edited more than 8,000 pages
of research.

9/89 to 4/90

Arista Foundation, New York, NY
Editorial Assistant
Assisted in various aspects of production of the foundation's
Journal of Aesthetics. Researched articles; maintained
database; corresponded with subscribers.

10/87 to 12/88

City Council, New York, NY
Volunteer
Worked in the offices of former City Councilwoman Renee
Salinger. Spoke with constituents, attended public hearings,
researched issues and wrote propositions for bills and
resolutions.

SKILLS:

IBM WordPerfect 5.0, Microsoft Word, type 70 wpm
Strong research and writing abilities

SPECIAL
ACHIEVEMENTS:

Recipient of four-year National Achievement Scholarship
for Outstanding Black student. Recipient of four-year
National Phi Delta Kappa, Inc. Scholarship.

REFERENCES:

On request.

JUDITH COLEMAN
38 Washington Avenue, Bethel, Connecticut 06804
203-555-5901

Education:

B.S., University of Connecticut, Storrs, CT
Hotel, Restaurant and Travel Administration
May 1992

Work Experience:

Camp Belair, Amherst, MA
Assistant Food Service Director   Summers '90, '91 and '92
- Supervised staff of 3 workers.
- Controlled inventories.
- Purchased food and checked-in supplies.
- Developed and prepared menus for 250 children ages 6 to 12.
- Controlled cash inflow and outflow.
- Voluntarily assisted in other camp functions.

University Hotel, Storrs, CT
Front Office Cashier   September '90 to May '91
- Directed day-to-day activities for hotel guests.
- Responsible for hotel operations: billing, checkout and front desk inquiries.
- Prepared pre-audit reports.

University of Connecticut, Storrs, CT
Dining Hall Worker   September '89 to May '91

Activities:

International Food Service Executive Association Student Chapter
Residence Hall Council

Skills:

BASIC computer programming, data entry on a PC,
certified in First Aid/CPR

References:

On request.

DANIEL M. LYONS

6 Three Rivers Road
Eugene, Oregon 97401
503-555-8275

EDUCATION:

Bachelor of Business Administration, May 1992
Concentration: Human Resources Management
University of Oregon, Eugene, Oregon

Associate of Arts, December 1987
Personnel Studies
Southwestern Oregon Community College, Coos Bay, Oregon

STUDIES:

Labor Relations - President of in-class union. Led group in contract negotiations and roleplaying involving the Big 3 Autoworkers.

Personnel Administration - Analyzed and created compensation and benefits packages as well as pension plans for employees of various corporations.

International Business - Researched monetary/trade policies and cultures of various countries.

Contemporary Problems in Human Resources - Researched and participated in lecture series on corporate ethics and business codes.

Organizational Development - Performed team-building exercises with emphasis on initiating change programs in corporations.

EMPLOYMENT:

Kellogs Catering, March 1989 - present full-time, summer part-time
Gresham, Oregon
Manager of Kitchen and Service Staff
Duties include arranging events to be coordinated with various reception halls. Monitor daily business activities, such as ordering, inventory control and customer service.

Pat's Tavern, April 1987 - September 1988
Coos Bay, Oregon
Assistant Kitchen Manager
Assignments included hiring and training of the staff. Position also included delegation of numerous tasks, including inventory ordering and scheduling of personnel.

INTERESTS:

Music, sports and travel

REFERENCES:

Furnished upon request

Marguerite Fordham

1616 Luna Drive
Beverly Hills, California 90210   213-555-6715

EDUCATION:

May 92	**University of California, Los Angeles, CA** BFA Degree Major: Illustration with emphasis in Photography
Spring 92	**Studio Art Centers International**, Florence, Italy
Summer 87	**Parsons School of Design**, The Dordogne and Paris, France

EXPERIENCE:

August -
December, 91

Robert Corrigan Studio, Los Angeles, CA
<u>Photographic Assistant</u>
Responsibilities included assisting on all levels of studio operations
and set-up. Assisted with studio shoots, film loading, clip testing,
sending and receiving film, contact and proof printing.

Summer 90

Elaine Gibb, Inc., Los Angeles, CA
<u>Studio Assistant</u>
Organized public relations mailings, established shoot dates, maintained
client relations; sent and received portfolios, compiled expenses.

Summer 89

Jim Henson Productions, Los Angeles, CA
<u>Creative Assistant</u>
Assisted in the creation and production of McDonald's "Happy
Meal" prototypes.

Summer 88

Kaye Bismark, Inc., Los Angeles, CA
<u>Design Assistant</u>
Assisted in preliminary stages of design projects including selection
of color palette and fabrics.

SKILLS:

On the Macintosh: PhotoShop, PageMaker, Illustrator and Word
Cameras: 4 X 5, 2 1/4, 35 mm
Strobe lighting, studio lighting and B/W retouching

ACTIVITIES:

Photo and Layout Editor, UCLA 1992 Yearbook

TRAVEL:

Italy, France, Spain and Colombia

LANGUAGES:

Fluent in French and Italian (speaking and reading)

**REFERENCES
& PORTFOLIO:** Furnished upon request.

JILL BELDEN

Current Address
616 Sanborn Street
College Station, TX 77840
409-555-3657

Permanent Address
972 Plantation Drive
Stillwater, OK 74074
405-555-9180

Objective: A challenging position in human resources that requires creativity and strong problem-solving skills.

Education: *May 1993*   *Texas A & M University, College Station, TX*
Bachelor of Science in Industrial and Labor Relations

Relevant Coursework: Personnel Management, Employee Benefits, Organizational Behavior, Employee Relations, Behavioral Differences, Statistics, Discrimination Law, Corporate Regulation, Business Law, Women in the Workplace, Personal Computing, Collective Bargaining and Public Speaking

Experience: *Assistant Case Administrator*
May 1992 to August 1992 American Arbitration Association, Brenham, TX
Coordinated caseload of arbitration cases in accordance with applicable law. Liaised between parties, their representatives and arbitrators. Responded to inquiries about AAA procedures and services. Attended hearings.

Recruiting Intern
November 1991 to January 1992 American Express, Beaumont, TX
Conducted a study of undergraduate universities for development of a marketing recruiting program. Learned the tactical and administrative aspects of recruitment coordination. Assisted recruiters with campus interviews.

Administrative Assistant
February 1989 to May 1990 Engineering Office, Texas A & M University
Worked in Dean's office on various projects including filing system reorganization, processing payroll, data entry on the PC; handled busy phones.

Activities & Awards: Member of Kappa Delta Sorority
Intramural Soccer and Volleyball
Rotary Scholarship

References: Furnished upon request.

CASPER T. BERGLIN
7899-22 Hewlett Court
Ahoskie, North Carolina 27910
919-555-3895

EDUCATION:

University of North Carolina at Chapel Hill, Chapel Hill, NC
BA International Studies with Honors, Minor in Political Science   May 1993
Honors: Dean's List 1989 - 1993
Institute for American Universities, Aix-en-Provence, France
(Study Abroad Program, Spring 1991)

EMPLOYMENT EXPERIENCE:

Democratic National Committee, Washington, D.C.   Spring & Summer 1992
Research Assistant
- Performed primary and secondary research on Republican presidential
  candidates.
- Assisted in preparation of weekly reports distributed to constituent groups.
- Participated in the development of on-line database for Presidential nominee.
- Served as aide at the 1992 Democratic National Convention in New York City.

U.S. Merchant Marine & Fisheries Committee, Washington, D.C.   Summer 1991
Intern
- Researched issues under committee jurisdiction of U.S. Representative
  Henry Muller.
- Coordinated special project ranking the coastal congressional districts accord-
  ing to land area, population and population density.
- Attended briefings, hearings and meetings concerning the activities of the
  committee.
- Computer literate on Macintosh. Handled various databases and spreadsheet
  applications.

ACTIVITIES:

Volunteer, Voluntary Workcamps Association of Ghana   Summer 1990
- Participated in the initial phases of construction of a medical clinic and
  research facility for a rural village in central Ghana.
Member, Phi Gamma Delta   *1989 to 1992*

REFERENCES:

Furnished upon request.

Juliette Adams
360 East 71st Street #15B
New York, NY 10027
212-555-1141

Education:	May 1992
	University of Arizona, Tucson, AZ
	B.A. Journalism, minor in Japanese
	44 credits completed at Soka University
	Hachioji, Tokyo, Japan

Experience: Summers 1991 & 1992
<u>Condé Nast Publications, New York, NY</u>
Part-time Assistant in all facets of magazine production:
- Merchandising   • Editorial
- Promotions   • Fashion
Worked at *Vogue, Vanity Fair, GQ, Self,* and *Glamour*

September 1991 to January 1992
<u>El Independiente, Tucson, AZ</u>
Assistant News Editor/Reporter
Managed news department and personnel as needed.
Wrote feature articles.

September 1990 to May 1991
<u>KPQR-TV Station, Tucson, AZ</u>
Intern.
Organized and delivered news scripts to all technical
and on-air talent. Worked the TelePromTer for the
10 o'clock news program.

Special Skills: Fluent in Japanese and Spanish.
Knowledge of MultiMate, Xywrite, Harvard writing
systems, typesetting equipment and typography.

References: On request.

MARGARET FOSTER
210 Maple Street
Arlington, Virginia 22205
703-555-1643

EDUCATION:

1992   George Washington University, Washington, D.C.
              B.A. in Journalism, French Minor
              Dean's List 1990, 1991, 1992
              Graduate Cum Laude
              Editor of student magazine "The Hill Dweller."

EXPERIENCE:

1992   Women's Wear Weekly, Washington, D.C.
              Internship
              Worked as Research Assistant to consumer reporter.
              Located items for Best Buys Feature; tested sample prod-
              ucts. Filled in as copy aide; assisted in production of news
              and fashion show.   Followed up news releases. Helped
              read and answer letters addressed to Fashion Questions
              column.

Summers   What's Happening Here?, Washington, D.C.
'90 & '91   Editorial Assistant
              Worked as right hand to Special Events Editor of weekly
              publication produced by Washington D.C. Visitor's
              Bureau. Assisted in writing, editing and layout. Followed
              up leads for feature articles. Interviewed event sponsors.
              Provided support to photographer on assignment at
              events and maintained contact with various cultural
              organizations.

SKILLS:

              Proficient on the Macintosh computer. Software
              includes: Microsoft Word, PageMaker, Illustrator and
              Digital Darkroom.

              Fluent in French; familiar with Italian.

REFERENCES:

              Available on request.

PAMELA SUMMERS
46 Ocean Parkway
Los Angeles, California 10623
213-555-4628

EDUCATION:

Georgetown University, Washington, D.C.   May 1993
B.S. in Languages; GPA 3.27 Dean's List Distinction
Major: Russian   Minor: Business
Languages: Fluency in Russian; knowledge of Italian, Spanish,
                      French and German
Business: International Business, Business Russian,
                      Macroeconomics, Microeconomics, Accounting

AWARDS:

Rhodes Scholarship Nominee

WORK EXPERIENCE:

February 1991 to present
SSCR/Bilingual Program, Washington, D.C.
Administrative Assistant/Special Projects
Research, review and edit bibliographies. Gather information and
write annotations for three soon-to-be published books.

Also do freelance editing and translation for foreign diplomats.

PERSONAL:

Have traveled extensively throughout Western Europe; some
travel in the former Soviet Union and South America.

REFERENCES:

Available on request (in English and in Russian).

Willing to relocate in the United States or abroad.

Naomi Martin

300 Allen Avenue
Pittsburgh, Pennsylvania
412-555-8376

Education: University of Chicago, Chicago, Illinois
Candidate of Juris Doctor   June 1992
Illinois Law Journal, Member   1990 - 92
Moot Court, Regionals: Oralist and Brief Writer 1991
International Law Society, Vice President   1991

University of Missouri, Springfield, Missouri
B.A. with Honors   1989
Major: American History

Employment: <u>Taft, Symons & Crabbe, Chicago, Illinois</u>   Summer 1991
Worked as *Paralegal* to a Partner in Antitrust and International
Corporate specialization. Performed research, heavy client
contact; thorough knowledge of legal document drafts, SEC
filings and registration statements.

<u>Marshall & Mattel, Pittsburgh, Pennsylvania</u>   Summer 1990
Functioned as temporary *Legal Secretary* to Litigation Partner.
Prepared legal documents; handled general administrative
duties such as word processing, heavy phones and client contact.

<u>Kendall's Junior Gymnastics, Pittsburgh, Pennsylvania</u>
Gymnastic Instructor   Summers '87, '88 & '89
Worked extensively with 6- and 7-year-old girls on various
gymnastic equipment. Coached students on dance routines and
balance beam events. Taught class in dance movement.

Activities: Women's Gymnastic Team
University of Missouri, Springfield, Missouri   1987 - 88
Competed on an athletic scholarship until knee injury.
Ranked #2 in Regionals and won the Skali Award for
innovative performance on floor routine.

References: Furnished upon request.

PAUL MARKS

3519 Palisades Avenue
Riverdale, New York 10463   *212-555-2080*

Education:

New York University, New York, New York   May 1992
Juris Doctorate
Graduated in top 15% of class
Recipient of American Jurisprudence Award

Emory University, Atlanta, Georgia
BA in Environmental Studies   January 1988

Bar Admission:

New York State Bar Exam to be taken September 1992.

Employment:

July 1992 to present
Office of the District Attorney, New York County
Responsible for the preparation and litigation of felony cases in
the Supreme Court. Draft and argue various motions; draft
appeals to the Supreme Court, Appellate Division, First Department.

March 1990 to September 1991
Klein, Covney & DeMuro, New York, NY
Drafted motions and assisted in the preparation of cases for trial.

Summers 1987 and 1988
Department of Health, Education & Welfare, Atlanta, Georgia
Drafted responses to appeals taken from administrative hearings
on disability benefits.

Activities:

Varsity tennis at Emory University

References:

Furnished on request.

CANDICE MONTGOMERY

901 Monticello Drive, #14C
Lisle, Illinois 60532
312-555-1793

EDUCATION

University of Illinois at Chicago, Chicago, IL
Major - Legal Studies, GPA - 3.7
Bachelor of Science, Cum Laude, May 1992
Achievements - Secretary of the Law Society 1991-92

WORK EXPERIENCE

Harvis, Taft & Duffey, Chicago, IL
Summers 1991 & 1992

Paralegal involved in a major litigation case. Responsible for reading all legal documents involved in the case and extracting all information that might be relevant. Also required to give a brief synopsis of the document's contents.

INTERNSHIP

City Planning Commission, Chicago, IL
1/92 - 6/92

Worked with Commissioner and Assistant Commissioner. Handled constituent complaints. Performed research concerning city government. Attended and helped plan and organize various functions involving the City Planner's Office.

SPECIAL SKILLS

Ability to brief cases, write legal memos and research case law and statutes.
Excellent at organizing, planning and executing tasks.
Self-starter with a lot of energy.
Knowledge of WordPerfect, Lotus 1-2-3, dBASE, and Westlaw.
Lived and attended school in Europe.

SPECIAL LAW CLASSES

Legal Research, Legal Writing, Law & Evidence, Constitutional Law, Law & Ethics and Criminal Law.

REFERENCES

Furnished upon request.

NICOLE MILLER
12 Laurel Valley
Bel Air, Maryland 2014
301-555-1583

Education:

1992   University of Maryland, College Park, MD
B.A. Liberal Arts with a Psychology concentration
Cumulative GPA 3.5   Dean's List four consecutive years

- Specialized in the assessment and evaluation of human behavior, thought patterns and communication. Worked with graduate students on psychological research and statistical analysis of results.
- Conducted studies in cognitive processes of the brain for senior thesis.
- Social Chairman and member of Alpha Epsilon Phi Sorority.
- Participated in philanthropic events including Dancers Against Cancer and Alcohol Awareness Week.

Employment Experience:

Summer 1992   Administrative Assistant, Van Dyne Corp., Baltimore, MD
Responsible for controlling and monitoring production, shipping, receiving and distribution of fashion merchandise from Far East vendors to domestic retail outlets. Worked with VP on sales figures, expenses and commissions. Gained proficiency in Lotus.

Summer 1991   Assistant Office Manager, Jaeger Enterprises, Aberdeen, MD
Assisted Office Manager and Sales team with telemarketing, purchasing, expediting orders, staff supervision, customer service and credit checks on new accounts.

Summer 1990   Administrative Assistant, Wendell & Tyler, Baltimore, MD
Performed a variety of office duties at medium-sized law firm. Aided attorneys in preparation of briefs; coordinated intricate schedule of monthly appointments; acted as liaison between clients and attorneys.

Summer 1989   Peer Advisor, University of Maryland, College Park, MD
Assisted undergraduate students in the selection of appropriate courses for their major. Designed and created plans to help students achieve their goals.

References: Furnished upon request.

LAWRENCE KNAPP

91 Swan Court
Bennington, VT 05291
802-555-5443

EDUCATION

Colorado State University, Fort Collins, CO, graduated December 1992
BA in Liberal Arts (Concentration: European History 1918-1945)
GPA 3.1, completed three school years in 18 months

Bennington College, Bennington, VT, September 1986 - June 1988

EXPERIENCE

On-Press, Boulder, CO
Summer 1991

Designed, printed and marketed logos on T-shirts. Created and marketed more than 15 designs.
Manufactured over 1,000 shirts for gross revenue of approximately $10,000. Marketed shirts wholesale to stores and retail to individuals. Used profits to finance personal living expenses and growth of company.

Campus Apparel, Fort Collins, CO
September 1988 - May 1989

Assistant store manager and salesman at large clothing store. Responsible for all daily store operations including inventory management, advertising and sales. Hired, trained and managed employees. Used salary to finance night classes.

Town & Country Painting, Bennington, VT
Summer 1988

Started entrepreneurial venture in house painting. Engaged business through extensive "mailbox marketing" effort and referrals. Painted two full exteriors and did other odd painting jobs for gross revenue of $6,500. Allocated and managed financial and material resources. Supervised three students.

Bennington Association for Retarded Citizens, Bennington, VT
Summer 1987

Volunteered assistance to the association. Responsible for managing up to eight clients at group homes. Assisted in client outings; supervised work duty in the light assembly area.

PERSONAL

Functionally fluent in French and Arabic
Extensive travel throughout the U.S., Middle East and Europe
Contributing editor to <u>Kaleidoscope</u>, a literary journal at Colorado State University
Enjoy tennis, squash, photography, reading history, and writing fiction

REFERENCES

Furnished upon request

ELIZABETH COSTELLO

68 June Street
Omaha, Nebraska 68108

402-555-2401

EDUCATION:

Yale University, New Haven, CT
BA in Business Administration, August 1992
Major: Management Information Systems
Minor: Consumer Marketing
Major Index: 3.67   Cumulative Index: 3.25

COMPUTER SKILLS:

Fully versatile on the IBM Personal Computer
WordPerfect 5.1, Lotus 1-2-3, dBase, Quattro, DisplayWrite IV,
COBOL, PageMaker with Windows

PROFESSIONAL EXPERIENCE:

Summer 1991
International Business Machines (IBM), White Plains, NY
Staff Assistant
Created documentation on DisplayWrite IV. Performed test case
typing for program analysis. Participated in pilot software
programs. Coordinated response to customer questionnaires;
analyzed data for product development division.

January 1990 to May 1992
Yale University, New Haven, CT
Payroll Clerk, University Staffing Services
Prepared prevailing wage documentation in accordance with
Connecticut State Labor Standards. Maintained and verified
employee work hours.

ACTIVITIES & INTERESTS:

MIS Club, Management & Marketing Club, Women's Chorus,
Women's Equestrian Team.
Extensive European travel; speak fluent Italian.

REFERENCES:

Available upon request.

LYNDA ANSBRO   29 Alan Road
914-555-2982   White Plains, NY 10603

Objective:

Entry-level position in sales, promotions or advertising.

Education:

Mercy College, Dobbs Ferry, New York
BBA Degree, Concentration in Marketing
May 1993

Related Coursework:

Women in Business   BASIC Programming
Sales & Promotions   Advertising
Consumer Behavior   Multinational Marketing

Field Experience:

Coordinated promotional campaign for White Plains Hospital's new perinatal building. Developed creative strategy, prepared 30-second radio commercial, utilized various types of direct mail, organized creative strategies aimed toward the recruitment of high school students for volunteer work.

Assisted in marketing research project for Mercy College Career Development Center: gathered pertinent, quantifiable data and recorded it.

Employment:

Helped finance college expenses through the following part-time jobs.
January 1991 to present
Finast Supermarket, White Plains, NY   Cashier

August 1989 to January 1991
The Pizza Plaza, White Plains, NY   Cashier/Waitress

Activities:

American Marketing Association
Mercy College Martial Arts Club

References: On request.

ARLENE C. NEWMEYER

Home Address: 84-84 Dalny Road, Jamaica, NY 11432   (718) 555-1904
School Address: 4309 Hortensia Avenue, San Diego, CA   92130   (714) 555-9952

JOB OBJECTIVE:
A position offering challenge and responsibility in consumer affairs, marketing or advertising research.

EDUCATION:
The University of California at San Diego
Graduating in May 1993 with a BA in Marketing and Consumer Behavior; Dean's List Distinction
Field of study includes: Marketing and Advertising Theory and Research, Economics, Business Law, Calculus,
Mass Communications, Statistics, Psychology, Sociology, and Research Methodology.

Also took related courses at UCLA and Berkeley: Social and Managerial Concepts in Marketing, Consumer
Behavior, Product Policy, Advertising Theory and Policies, Sales Force Management, Marketing Research.

MARKETING PROJECTS/COURSE ASSIGNMENTS:
- Children and Advertising -- Selling to the Sandbox Set
- Marketing Research -- Cash vs. Credit Retail Analysis
- Portrayal of Women in Magazine Advertising
- Persuasive Impact of Liquor Ads in Print Media
- The Male Contraceptive Pill: Product Development and Marketing/Advertising Strategies

SUMMER WORK EXPERIENCE:
1992   Califdata Corporation, San Diego, CA
Administrative Assistant in Sales Department. Trained in basic sales and organizational procedures.
Responsible for recordkeeping, expense reports, PR, correspondence and inventory updates.

1991   Graham Mills, La Jolla, CA
Back Office Sales Assistant. Responsible for billing, orders, inventory and shipping.

1990   The Press Club, San Diego, CA
Replaced full-time Secretary to Public Relations Director during Secretary's maternity leave.
General office work and personal computer projects utilizing WordPerfect 5.0.

ACTIVITIES:
Volunteer Cook for San Diego Soup Kitchen (feeding the homeless)

REFERENCES:
On request.

SYDNEY ORLOFF
107 East Byron #2A
Keyport, NJ 07735
908-555-1639

EDUCATION:

Louisiana State University, Baton Rouge, LA
Graduate School of Arts and Sciences
Master of Science in Applied Mathematics
August 1992

New York University, New York, NY
College of Arts and Sciences
Bachelor of Arts in Mathematics
June 1990

WORK EXPERIENCE:

Teaching Assistant   8/91 - 5/92
Louisiana State University, Baton Rouge, LA
Taught Business Math and College Algebra in
classes of approximately 30 students; tutored
students individually in math; proctored
placement exams.

Personnel/Payroll Clerk   4/90 - 8/90
U.S. Bureau of the Census, New York, NY
Processed and audited payroll and personnel
forms. General bookkeeping and data entry.

Math Tutor   9/86 - 6/90
New York University, New York, NY
School of Education, Health, Nursing & Art
Professions -- Higher Education Opportunity Program.
Substituted for instructors in the program.
Tutored high school students in all levels of math;
assisted them in their preparation for SATs and New
York State Regents Exams. Tutored NYU students in
Calculus and Business Math.

ADDITIONAL INFORMATION:
Passed Actuarial Exam 100
Licensed New York State Notary Public

REFERENCES: On request.

DANIEL HANERFORD
29 Rockland Avenue
Hartford, Connecticut
(203) 555-1415

EDUCATION:

February 1993   Fordham University, Bronx, NY
B.A., Medieval and Renaissance Studies

May 1989   Dean Junior College, Franklin, MA
A.A. in Liberal Arts

WORK EXPERIENCE:

July 1989 to present   Teller, Citibank, Bronx, NY
–Train and evaluate teller trainees.
–Perform all bank teller functions.
–Prepare branch currency reports.

September '91 to April '92   Administrative Assistant
Grant Fielding Architectural Project
(Cooperative work experience/course credit received)
–Translated artist's notes from French to English; typed manuscript.
–Organized and catalogued artist's memorabilia and material.
–Interpreted artist's work according to imaginary architecture and Augustinian philosophy.

SKILLS:

Read and speak French; reading knowledge of Latin and Italian. Microsoft Word on the Mac.

REFERENCES:

Available upon request.

MAUREEN SHAUNESSEY
1645 Diane Court
Oak Brook, Illinois 60521
312-555-6391

EDUCATION:

Northwestern University, Evanston, Illinois
Bachelor of Arts, Metropolitan Studies   May 1992
GPA 3.0/4.0
Recipient of Knights of Columbus Academic Scholarship

CAMPUS ACTIVITIES:

College of Arts & Sciences Student Council
Yearbook Committee/Advertising Coordinator
Leader, AIDS Walkathon Project
Tutor for Hazlewood Junior High School, Evanston, IL
    (Assist 7th graders with Social Studies curriculum)

EMPLOYMENT:

Summers 1991 & 1992 (also semester breaks)
Sales Associate
<u>Marshall Field & Company Department Store, Chicago, IL</u>
Processed all cash purchases in the Leather Handbag department.
Became familiar with stock to facilitate customer shopping.
Assisted manager with sales promotions.
Arranged merchandise in display cases.

Summer 1990
Administrative Assistant
<u>Haskins & Rick, Oak Brook, IL</u>
General secretarial support for small law firm. Assisted Partner's
Secretary with preparation of cases for trial, drafting of legal
documents and reception. Performed word processing and spread-
sheet functions. (Knowledge of WordPerfect and Lotus 1-2-3.)

REFERENCES:

Available on request.

JACKSON LUNSFORD

1122 Naples Terrace   Home: 302-555-6329
Dover, Delaware 19901   Campus: 603-555-9513

EDUCATION:

Dartmouth College, Hanover, New Hampshire
BA in Music (Concentration Operatic Studies)   May 1993

GENERAL BACKGROUND:

- Conducted in-depth research, wrote and edited articles of an investigative nature about world news, art and politics for the *Dartmouth Icon*.
- Managed the distribution of a monthly campus newsletter; updated mailing list database and maintained financial records.
- Mounted campus advertising campaigns as student liaison with college administration.
- Worked closely with various conductors, managed a small staff and played an integral role in the success of a seasonal music festival.
- Performed leading campus roles staged with full orchestra.
- Held recitals for the Dartmouth student body.

EMPLOYMENT HISTORY:

Teaching Assistant, Dartmouth College Music Dept., Hanover, NH   1/'92-5/'93
Intern, Baltimore Opera Association, Baltimore, MD   Summer '91
Score Reader, Baltimore Opera Association, Baltimore, MD   Summer '90
Concert Committee Assistant, Dartmouth College, Hanover, NH   9/'89-5/'91

CAMPUS ACTIVITIES:

The Dartmouth Icon -- Editorial Board Member & Culture Editor
Dartmouth Conservative Society -- President '92, Treasurer '90
Dartmouth Gentlemen's Club -- Member

MUSIC ACTIVITIES:

Dartmouth College Choir
Dartmouth Opera Workshop
Dartmouth College Madrigal Singers (traveled extensively throughout U.S.)

AWARDS:

The Treble Clef, awarded by the Dartmouth Music Department to the senior who has made outstanding contributions to the program.

REFERENCES:

Performance and work references on request.

WAYNE M. FEIFFER
7301 Mullins Drive, Apt. #136
Houston, Texas 77081
713-555-8675

EDUCATION:

Oberlin College, Oberlin, Ohio
Bachelor of Arts in Music
May 1993
Major: Piano Performance
Minor: Music Therapy

EMPLOYMENT:

Part-time while in school -- worked 15 hours weekly while carrying full course load.
Children's Village, Oberlin, Ohio
January 1992 to June 1992
- Participated in music therapy sessions for 7 autistic and 16 physically and/or emotionally handicapped children.
- Inspired an appreciation of music by encouraging instrument play, sing-alongs and dance movement classes.
- Promoted self-awareness through music.
- Introduced children to the works of Mozart, Handel and Strauss.

Saint John's Episcopal Church, Oberlin, Ohio
March 1990 to December 1991
- Supervised Children's Choir
- Played organ for two Sunday services weekly.

ADDITIONAL
MUSIC SKILLS:

Piano	Organ	Harp
Guitar	Banjo	Violin

REFERENCES:

On request. (Willing to audition or forward recital tapes.)

Suzanne Backus
29 Hemlock Avenue
Dobbs Ferry, New York 10522
914-555-2139

Education:

University of California at Berkeley   1993
Bachelor of Science in Nursing

Employment:

Field Study Assignment:
St. Mary's Hospital, Berkeley, CA   1/92 to 8/93
- Worked in Cardiac Unit assisting with general patient care.
- Took histories, kept charts, prepared patients for tests and treatments.

Laboratory Assistant
Los Angeles General Hospital, Los Angeles, CA   5/91 to 8/91
- Assisted in report production.
- Prepared slides for testing.
- Maintained records of lab tests for miscellaneous research.
- Cleaned and checked equipment.

Activities:

- UCLA Student Nurse Association
- Para-tech Sky Diving Team
- Residence Council Representative
- Intramural sports: racquetball and tennis

Languages:

Conversational Spanish

References:

Available on request.

ANNA SUAREZ
98 Painted Sky Road
Phoenix, Arizona
602-555-1151

Career Objective: Dietitian

Education: May 1993
<u>B.S., Michigan State University</u>, East Lansing, Michigan
Major: Nutrition
Minor: Chemistry
Dean's List 4 consecutive years

Coursework: Emphasis of study was on commercial food processing, specialization in food preparation for the elderly.

Experience: Summer 1992
<u>Masonic Temple</u>, Detroit, Michigan
Dietary Intern
Planned menus and supervised meal preparation.

Summer 1991
<u>Marlboro State Hospital</u>, Marlboro, Michigan
Helped translate convalescent diets into actual meals. Selected and delivered special meals to restricted-diet patients.

Summer 1990
<u>Mundy's Restaurant</u>, East Lansing, Michigan
Short-order cook and waitress.

Interests: Breadmaking, camping, horseback riding

References: On request.

Madeline McShane
45-78 #5F Crooked Hill Byway
Linton, Indiana 47441   **812-555-2341**

EDUCATION: *The Philadelphia Institute, Philadelphia, PA*
                  Litigation Management Program
                  Diploma awarded: May 1992

                  Indiana University, Bloomington, IN
                  Bachelor of Arts in Political Science
                  May 1991   Graduated Magna Cum Laude

                  Student Exchange Program
                  Catholic University of Puerto Rico, Summer 1989

EMPLOYMENT: **Academic Assistance Program, Bloomington, IN**
                  Administrative Intern   *June 1991 to August 1991*
                  ❑ Supervised 13 students, grades 7 & 8, at local schools.
                  ❑ Assisted with concerns and questions.
                  ❑ Coordinated educational and social programs.
                  ❑ Monitored study hours.

                  University Law Library, Bloomington, IN
                  Library Page   *August 1988 - May 1989*
                  ❑ Filed books; assisted at circulation desk.
                  ❑ Coordinated inventory of archives.
                  ❑ Located reference material; assisted students with
                    microfiche equipment.

VOLUNTEER EXPERIENCE:
                  The Pennsylvania Prison Society   *Feb. 92 - May 92*
                  Worked as liaison between inmates and administration.

                  Coalition for the Homeless   *Jan. 91 - April 91*
                  Worked in soup kitchen; assisted with thrift shop
                  merchandise; participated in fund-raising events.

SKILLS: Bilingual Spanish, WordPerfect, Westlaw

REFERENCES: On request.

Emmaline Westervelt
5 James Avenue
Chattanooga, Tennessee 37401
615-555-1580

Education:	Syracuse University (School of Management), Syracuse, NY	May 1993
	Bachelor of Science: Personnel & Industrial Relations	

Projects:
–Designed wage regression schedule to standardize job pay grades for a corporation.
–Developed a benefits program for a corporation with 25 employees (benefits package included Eldercare Fund, Profit Sharing, HMO and Daycare facilities.)

Experience:

MCI, Philadelphia, Pennsylvania
Telemarketer   Summer 1992
–Participated in training session that detailed history of MCI and the psychology of the consumer.
–Promoted MCI to 400 potential buyers daily.

Benjamin Franklin Medical Center, Philadelphia, Pennsylvania
Summer Intern   Summer 1991
–Participated in annual Blood Drive.
–Assisted with clerical and reception duties and special projects.
–Calculated time pay cards and wrote up totals for bookkeeping.

Ester Roberts Fashions, Chattanooga, Tennessee
Salesperson   Summers '89 & '90
–Opened and closed shop.
–Handled monthly inventory count.
–Designed merchandise displays in store windows.
–Handled on-the-floor sales.
–Utilized cash register.
–Everyday customer service.

Activities:	1990 - 1992	Society for Human Resources Management
	1989 - 1991	Sorority, Sigma Delta Tau
		–Alcohol Policies/Rape Awareness Chairperson
		–Member of the Selection Committee
	1989 - 1990	Syracuse University Ski Team

References: Available on request.

JANICE S. MORGAN
201 West 81st Street, Apt. 5R
New York, NY 10024
212-555-9284

EDUCATION
Vassar College, Poughkeepsie, NY
BA in Philosophy, May 1992
Additional course work in History and English
Senior Essay: Prostitution: A Study in Social Morality and the Law

WORK EXPERIENCE
The Pennywhistle Papers, New York, NY   Summer 1991 and 1992
Clerical Assistant, Advertising Department
Responsible for preparation of advertisements to run weekly. Worked with desktop publishing/
graphic artists team. Functioned as liaison between Advertising Sales and Production staff.

Merrill Photo Supplies, New York, NY   Summer 1990
Salesperson
Sold, ordered and serviced cameras.

VOLUNTEER EXPERIENCE
The Department of Human Resources, Poughkeepsie, NY   1992
Working with government social worker, assisted with court cases for children placed in foster
homes.

Congressional Intern, Washington, D.C.   Summer 1989
The Honorable John K. Devaney (D., WV)
Researched bills and constituent requests.

ACTIVITIES
The Miscellany News (Weekly Student Newspaper)
Managing Editor   1992
Recruited and maintained staff of writers, artists and photographers. Edited and proofed copy.
Supervised layout and production of each issue.

Photography Editor   1991
Responsible for developing, printing and assigning photographs for each issue. Assisted with
production. Contributing writer.

INTERESTS
Creative writing, whitewater rafting and photography.

REFERENCES
Furnished upon request.

Heidi Ruland
879 Robin's Nest Way
Toledo, Ohio
419-555-4329

Education:
1993

University of Wisconsin, Milwaukee, Wisconsin
Bachelor of Science in Physical Therapy
State Certified & Licensed

Activities:

Dean's List   GPA 3.33
Student Government, Assistant Budget Director
Resident Advisory Council, Chairperson
Freshman Biology Tutor
Women's Swim Team

Field Experience:
1/92 - 6/92

St. Joseph's Memorial Hospital, Milwaukee, Wisconsin
Student Intern/Children's Ward
* Participated in postoperative and long-term therapy
  with preadolescents.
* Assisted with prosthetic acclimatization program.
* Worked with juvenile patients on small motor
  coordination.

Employment:
Summers
1990 & 1991

Hitherhills State Park, Montauk, New York
First Aid Station
* Aided attending physician at summer resort.
* Managed inventory supply and assisted in
  routine medical procedures.

References:

On request.

KATE PICKARD
128 Paul Revere Road
Cambridge, Massachusetts 02138
617-555-1781

EDUCATION:

<u>Tufts University, Medford, MA</u>   1992
BA in Political Science, Dean's List
Peace and Justice Studies Certificate
Coursework in Law, Sociology, Politics and Education.

<u>La Sorbonne, Institut d'Etudes Sciences Politiques</u>   1990 - 1991
Paris, France (Junior year abroad program)
Coursework in International Relations, History and Art.
All lectures and courses conducted in French.

<u>Università per Stranieri, Perugia, Italy</u>   Summer 1991
Intensive language and culture program.

EXPERIENCE:

<u>Department of the Attorney General, Boston, MA</u>   Spring 1992
Cooperative Work Program/Internship
Investigated nature of consumer complaints and resolved cases as a
Mediator between complainants and merchants in the Consumer
Complaint Division. Extensive implementation of the Consumer
Protection Act, Landlord/Tenant Regulation, Motor Vehicle Regulations,
Lemon Laws and Small Claims Court procedures.

<u>Friendly's, Cambridge, MA</u>   1989 - 1990
Waitress for family-style restaurant.

LANGUAGE SKILLS:

Fluent French; conversational Italian

REFERENCES:

Upon request.

Carolyn Lyndsey
740 East Gun Hill Road
Bakersfield, California 93309
805-555-3987

Education:
University of Georgia, Atlanta, GA   January 1993
B.S. Psychology -- Mental Health
Dean's List
Federal Mental Health Grant Recipient
Mary Bethune Social Science Award Nominee
Member of Psychology Society
Member of Black Women of Georgia

Experience:
Health Insurance Plan, Atlanta, GA   May 1991 to present
<u>Records Coordinator</u>   (1/92 to present)
Maintain enrollment reports; update admissions records for Dept. of Mental
Health. Perform statistical analyses for quarterly reports. Assisted with
reorganization of Records Room for greater efficiency. Corrected misfilings.
Microfiched archive material.
<u>Census Taker</u>   (5/91 to 12/92)
Collected data from 60 doctors; performed statistical analyses for HEW-
sponsored Medicare time study.

Volunteer Experience:
Baycove Children's Center   Summers 1989 & 1990
Boston, Massachusetts
<u>Mental Health Counselor</u>
Participated in volunteer care of emotionally disturbed children residing at
special treatment center for abuse victims. Planned day trip activities.
Assisted with curriculum development. (Earned degree credit.)

Botanical Institute   1991 & 1992
University of Georgia, Atlanta
Performed plant maintenance. Worked extensively with rare orchids.

References:
Available through University of Georgia Placement Office, 404-555-1750.

Frances J. Worthington

318 Market Drive
Reston, Virginia 22091
703-555-5528

EDUCATION:

Skidmore College, Saratoga Springs, NY
B.A. – May 1992
Major: Public Administration   Minor: Religion

HONORS:

Phi Beta Kappa; National Honor Society
Periclean Society; Skidmore Honor Society
Cumulative GPA 3.69 on a 4.0 scale

LEADERSHIP EXPERIENCE:

Representative, College Government
Skidmore College
Integrated cross-cultural concerns to promote more diversified campus curriculum and projects. Assisted Admissions Office with recruitment of multi-ethnic students.
1991 - 1992

Co-Director of Executive Task Force on Campus Planning
Skidmore College
Analyzed needs of student body regarding key academic and social issues. Presented summary of findings and recommendations to the college president. Assisted with long-term architectural plans.
1990 - 1992

Director, Recycling Program, Skidmore College
Developed and implemented first waste materials re-cycling program for Skidmore College. Recruited and trained professionals and student workers to operate the program. Produced 27% savings of resource utilization by end of fourth year.
1989 - 1992

INTERESTS:

World travel, tennis, classical music.

REFERENCES:

Furnished upon request.

VANDER TYLER
171 North Jackson Street #4D
Birmingham, Alabama 35203
205-555-6629

EDUCATION:

May 1992   Masters of Public Health
            Columbia University School of Public Health, New York, NY

May 1990   Bachelor of Arts in Biology
            Johns Hopkins University, Baltimore, MD

EMPLOYMENT HISTORY:

June '90   The City of New York, Department of Human Resources
to present   South Bronx, New York
              Administrative Aide
              • Assisted in the implementation of outreach program for
                substance abusers.
              • Screened and interviewed clients at intake division of
                welfare center.
              • Analyzed demographic trends using statistical models.
              • Compiled data for Administrator.

June '88   Johns Hopkins University, Baltimore, Maryland
to May '90   Lab Assistant
              • Analyzed actin and myosin muscle fibers in rabbits using
                gel electrophoresis techniques.
              • Also worked in Gene Deregulation Research -- duties
                included preparation of petri dishes and agar plates
                and analysis of data.

SKILLS:

Basic knowledge of medical terminology
Knowledge of MacWrite and Excel on the Macintosh

REFERENCES:

Furnished upon request.

Grace Whitler
98 Longwood Drive
Phoenix, Arizona 85073
602-555-1151

Education:

January 1993
B.A. Temple University, Philadelphia, PA
Major: Radio/Television/Film
Minor: Psychology

Work History:

February 1992 to June 1993
America Broadcasts -- The TV Museum, Philadelphia, PA
Curatorial Assistant (Work/Study Program)
- Assisted Curatorial Department with its plans and exhibitions.
- Inventoried donations; worked on acquiring new material.
- Assisted in the creation and editing of seminar tapes.
- Answered research inquiries.

December 1990 to May 1991
W-DMAT Radio, Philadelphia, PA
Market Researcher
- Surveyed local households regarding listening habits.

Achievements:

Dean's List, graduated Magna Cum Laude
Worked and studied in London through Temple's Study Abroad Program
Did voice-overs on video exhibits for special TV festivals.
Wrote TV reviews for Student Newspaper, "The Clarion."
Volunteer for Meals-On-Wheels Program.

References:

Available upon request.

JANINE ALLENWOOD
1390 Mimosa Terrace #5C
St. Paul, Minnesota   55149

612-555-3291

EDUCATION

1992   <u>M.S.W., Columbia School of Social Work</u>
New York, New York

1990   <u>B.S., Social Services, University of Minnesota</u>
St. Paul, Minnesota

1986   <u>A.A.S., Sociology, Minneapolis Community College</u>
Minneapolis, Minnesota

EXPERIENCE

1/91 to present   *Family Caseworker, Catholic Churches, St. Paul, Minnesota*
Interview patients and their families at St. Anne's Hospital
to ascertain the needs for home health care, child care
assistance, ongoing therapy and financial help.

7/88 to 8/90   *Recreation Coordinator, The Swallows Geriatric Facility*
St. Paul, Minnesota
Worked extensively with 225 elderly residents. Instituted
"Grandparents Program" uniting 36 residents with local
elementary school children from dysfunctional families.

5/85 to 6/87   *Publicity Assistant, Multiple Sclerosis Society*
Minneapolis, Minnesota
Responsible for gathering information to establish branch
chapters. Duties included handling of news releases, generation
of press kits and contacts with chapter members. Heavy
involvement with local merchants for national telethon.

ADDITIONAL INFORMATION

- Volunteer member of Crisis Hotline (campus telephone
  support group)
- Financed 60% of all educational costs through work/study,
  grants and academic scholarships.

REFERENCES

Furnished on request.

ARTHUR OWENS
58 Black Oak Court
Scotch Plains, New Jersey 07076
201-555-3479 or 201-555-7843

EDUCATION:

Bachelor of Arts Degree awarded May 1992
Gettysburg College, Gettysburg, Pennsylvania
Major: Sociology   Minor: Psychology

COURSE WORK:

Human Information Processing, Introduction to Measurements and Statistics,
Calculus, Social Psychology, Sociology and the Family, Experimental Methods,
Assessment of Personality and Intelligence, Abnormal Psychology

COLLEGE ACTIVITIES:

1992   Executive Office of Phi Gamma Delta
        Committee member of team selected to design and administer the judicial
        and financial policies of 72-member fraternity and house.
        Supervised Philanthrophy and Scholarship Committees.
1992   Senior Class Cabinet
1991   Candidate, Student Leadership Conference
1990   Steward of Phi Gamma Delta; controlled food usage.
        Answered to brotherhood's comments and criticisms.
        Supervised house landscaping project.
89-92   Member of Gettysburg Soccer Team

WORK HISTORY:

Summer 1991 & 1992   First Security Corporation, Woodbridge, NJ
                          Security Guard, Woodbridge Center (Mall)

Summer 1989 & 1990   Chem Lawn, Plainfield, NJ
                          Lawn Care Worker

REFERENCES:

Available upon request.

MARTHA HIGGINS
21 Clare Drive
Melville, New York 11747
516-555-4498

OBJECTIVE:

Special Education or Elementary Education Teacher

EDUCATION:

C. W. Post College, Greenvale, NY
B.S. Special Education/Elementary Education
May 1992
3.2 GPA

CERTIFICATION:

New York State Provisional Teaching Certificate
Qualified for:

- Special Education -- Nursery School through 12th Grade
  Educable Mentally Retarded, Trainable Mentally Retarded,
  Learning Disabled or Emotionally Disturbed
- Elementary Education -- Nursery School through Sixth Grade

FIELD EXPERIENCE:

Special Education Student Teaching
Circle Hill Elementary School, Commack, NY
January 1992 to May 1992

Elementary School Student Teaching
Bellrose Elementary School, East Northport, NY
January 1991 to May 1991

WORK EXPERIENCE:

Summers 1990 - 1992 Commack Public Library, Commack, NY
Summer 1989 - MacDonald's, Northport, NY

REFERENCES:

Contact Career Services Center, C. W. Post College, 516-555-1200

MEGAN ADLER
98 Longwood Acres
Plano, Texas 75074
214-555-6609

EDUCATION:

Texas Christian University, Fort Worth, Texas
Major: Speech Communication 3.4 / 4.0 GPA
Minor: English as a Second Language
Degree: Bachelor of Science, May 1992

Institut für Europäische Studien, Vienna, Austria
January 1991 to May 1991

REPRESENTATIVE COURSEWORK:

Organizational Communication   Advanced Public Speaking
Marketing Management   Broadcast Speech
Linguistics & Language   Teaching Methods for ESL

EMPLOYMENT EXPERIENCE (earned approximately 40% of school expenses):

Career Blazers Temporary Personnel, Fort Worth, Texas
June 1991 to August 1992
Various positions involving data entry, direct customer service and word
processing.

Balloon Bouquets, Fort Worth, Texas
August 1989 to December 1990
Delivered balloons to campus residents.
Took phone orders.
Assisted with balloon decorations for catered affairs.

Cuskatoy Country Club, Plano, Texas
June 1989 to August 1989
Waitress

HONORS & ACTIVITIES:

Sigma Phi Chi (Speech Honors Society)
Kappa Delta Sorority (Social Chairman)
Women in Communications
Semester abroad (Austria)

COMPUTER SKILLS:

WordPerfect 5.1   Lotus 1-2-3   dBase IV

REFERENCES: On request.

TODD CRINKLE
RFD #5
Cumberland Hill, Rhode Island 02864
401-555-8796

Career Objective:

Entry opportunity in Sports Information or Public Information office at the collegiate or professional level.

Education:

Western Connecticut State University
Danbury, Connecticut
B.A., January 1993
Major: Sports Information
Minor: Physical Education

Sports-related Experience:
9/91 - 12/92   Western Connecticut State University
Assistant to Director of Sports Information
- Wrote and disseminated hometown and weekly press releases.
- Maintained statistics for football, men and women's basketball, baseball and softball.

Work Experience:
5/89 to 8/89   F & L Landscaping Services, Newport, RI
and
5/90 to 8/90   - Participated in all phases of lawn and garden maintenance: mowing, weeding, pruning, planting, fertilizing and design.
- Clients included residences and businesses.

Activities: Intramural sports (baseball and golf)
Certified scuba diver

PC Skills: WordPerfect, Excel, PowerPoint

References: On request.

KATHLEEN O'DWYER

5 Diane Court
Oyster Bay, New York 11771
516-555-1082

Education: Received a B.S. from Ohio University in June 1992
Major: Telecommunications
Concentration: Journalism and German

Work Experience: ***Good Morning America***, *Intern*, New York, NY
Spring 1992 - Serviced on-air quotes, updated press lists, produced newspaper clips for distribution, assisted with on-air promos, and dealt with ABC affiliates and viewers.

Lance, Frayne & Harvey, *Administrative Assistant*, New York, NY
Winter 1991-Worked exclusively with the president and vice president in preparing daily memos, letters, price lists, and management reports. Translated French correspondence. Assisted customers with their questions.

Merrill Lynch, *Administrative Assistant*, Cleveland, OH
Fall 1990 - Quoted daily gains/losses on the NBI system, worked on clients' profiles, distributed monthly newsletters, and directed customers' calls.

NBC WKYC-TV, *Production Intern*, Cleveland, OH
Winter 1990 - Worked on a two-hour substance abuse Prime Time Special, researched many topics for public affairs programs, handled guest booking and relations.

Special Skills: WordPerfect 5.0/ 5.1, Macintosh, IBM, Database, Excel, and NBI
Typing 40-45 wpm
Knowledge of German and French (speaking, reading, and writing)

Memberships: RTNDA, IRTS, and NATAS

References: Upon request

BRENDA MURPHY
401-555-4057

135 Ocean Drive
Newport, Rhode Island 02840

Education:

Rhode Island School of Design, Providence, Rhode Island
B.A. Textile Design   January 1993

Related Coursework:

- Concepts in Fashion
- Textiles for Interiors
- General Retailing
- Visual Merchandising
- History of Fashion Design
- Merchandising Math
- Surface Pattern Design
- The Study of Color & Light

Special Skills:

Working knowledge of Design Graphics Software: Weave Planner
Software by AVL Looms & Loom Software by William Jones.

Internship:

Professor's Assistant -- Textiles for Interiors Class
January 1992 to August 1992
Aided professor in the instruction of the class; graded papers; planned
field trips to museums.

Employment:

The High Sign, Providence, Rhode Island
January 1990 to May 1990
Sales Associate for Women's Retail Fashions
- Responsible for extensive sales and customer service.
- Handled window design, ordering, inventory control and cash register.

Camp Wanakegan, Newport, Rhode Island
Summers 1989 and 1990
Camp Counselor; Arts & Crafts Leader
- Supervised and provided care for youth in overnight camp.
- Developed arts and crafts projects for over 300 children.
- Ordered and purchased art supplies.

References & Art Portfolio:

On request.
Textile designs available in slide format for mailing.

THE JOB SEARCH

Your job search begins in your own backyard! Of all the various job sources, the most convenient—and at times the best—are your friends, relations, and neighbors. Anyone you know, including your doctor, dentist, former Scout leader, den mother or father might be the very person to furnish you with the lead you've been looking for. So when you're looking for a job, don't keep it a secret. The philosophy of your campaign is to let as many people as possible know that you are job hunting.

Don't be secretive or embarrassed about asking for help. Enlist the support of as many people as you possibly can. People like to help. Turn the situation around; if you were working and a friend or aquaintance asked you for help, wouldn't you be eager to assist in any way you could?

Everyone has looked for a job at one time or another and therefore is able to become very empathetic toward a job seeker—especially when it's the very first after graduation. Don't be shy and, whenever possible, give the person you've spoken to a copy or two of your résumé. You might be very surprised to know how fast résumés get circulated.

Often companies have the policy of posting new openings on the company bulletin board before the jobs are advertised or listed with employment agencies. The reason for this is that companies really do want to promote from within; often no outside person is interviewed for the opening unless no one on staff either wants the job or is qualified for it. Companies prefer to hire someone recommended by an employee rather than a complete stranger.

CLASSIFIED ADS

Read the ads! Not only on Sunday, but every day! There's a good chance of your finding the very job of your dreams, but there is also a wealth of information about the job market in your part of the country.

College grads often make the mistake of only looking under "college grads" or "trainee" and are discouraged to find few if any listings.

When searching the ads, consider every job title from A through Z. A perfect job may be listed under Administrative Assistant, Gal/Guy Friday,

Secretary, Research Assistant, Paralegal, Public Relations Assistant, Assistant Editor, Editorial Assistant, Salesperson, Publisher's Assistant, etc. A Comptroller's Assistant might very well be a Management Trainee, and a secretarial position in advertsising is very possibly an opportunity to learn to be a copywriter. Be sure to read not only the job title but the copy describing the position and the qualifications required.

If you find an ad that interests you and you have some but not all of the requirements, it's worth investigating. More often than not, positions are filled by people who can do the job but don't possess all the requirements listed by the company. When a company decides to add to its staff, they will prepare the job specs for the ideal candidate. As time goes by, it becomes more and more important to fill that job. The company may not, however, be getting the response to the ad that they expected.

The employer then realizes that the ad was not realistic, and Personnel will drop some of the specs and just find someone who can do the job. The same applies to salaries—a job may be listed for $18,500 and ultimately be filled for $21,000.

Since you are looking for the best job possible, it is advisable to explore as many opportunities as you can. Go out on as many interviews as feasible to learn as much as you can about each job offered. Then, after careful consideration of each job together with all its benefits, opportunities and ramifications, accept the one which most closely resembles what you are looking for.

Be sure to follow specific directions for each particular ad. If a phone number is listed, you'd be correct in inferring that they want you to call and set up an appointment. Do so. Don't arrive without warning. You might think it shows enthusiasm; it doesn't. It shows a lack of concern and can only waste your and the interviewer's time.

If a box number is listed, reply by sending your résumé with a cover letter. (Cover letters will be discussed in Chapter 7.)

Don't be discouraged if you don't get immediate results. At times, as much as three months elapses before you receive a response from your résumé. This is par for the course!

Remember, job hunting is harder, more traumatic, and more frustrating than working, but once you find a job, the weeks or months of anxiety will be forgotten immediately.

While studying the want ads, you can measure how realistic you are in your expectations. Look closely at the salaries offered for recent college graduates. Is your minimum in line? If not, do a little thinking and bring your hopes closer to reality.

Are you one of the many college students who is "philosophically" opposed to typing, although you find that many of the most interesting job listings require typing? If so, we are very sympathetic, and we are aware that no one goes to college to become a typist, but to refuse to use your typing, or to determine *not* to acquire such a marketable skill, would be doing yourself a tremendous disservice.

Companies are well aware that a college graduate will not be happy in either a clerk-typist or straight typist job, and they realize that an unhappy employee, in all probability, will not work out. Employers are, without exception, very cost conscious. Hiring and "breaking in" a new employee is an expensive process for a company. In addition to the clerical costs of setting up a new personnel file, adding to the insurance roster, setting up payroll cards, etc., there is also the fact that many offices believe few employees can actually *earn* their salaries until having worked for that employer for at least three months. One of the functions of the personnel department, department heads, and anyone involved in recruiting is the avoidance of unnecessary expense by making very sure that the job specifications are correct—and that the mistake of hiring candidates who are either underqualified or overqualified does not occur.

It is difficult for a recent graduate to distinguish between those jobs requiring typing that are actually dead ends and those jobs that offer an opportunity for growth and advancement. A further complication is that interviewers don't like to make absolute promises of just where a job will lead. Though an interviewer can learn a great deal about you from meeting you and studying your résumé, he or she still doesn't have enough information to give you a guarantee that in six months you'll be doing "whatever." Only time will tell how stable you are. Will you usually be prompt? Will you be absent more than would be predictable? How well will you get along with the staff? Are you as reliable as you appear? Until that is known, there can be no promises.

Fortunately, the decision as to whether or not a particular job has potential is actually not as esoteric as we may have implied. Remember, the interviewer's job is to hire the very best person he or she can possibly find who will be an asset not only in the short term, but in long-term employment. The interviewer is trained to *know* that college grads are looking for a job with potential; so if you receive an offer you can be reasonably sure the job has career possibilities and will offer much responsibility and opportunity for advancement.

While browsing through the classified ads, make special note of all information pertaining to employment agencies. Many agencies run "institutional ads," usually close to the beginning of the want ads or classifieds. The institutional ads give the name and address of the agency and a representative listing of jobs they are trying to fill. Studying these ads closely will help you decide which of these agencies might be helpful to you. An agency advertisement might make note of the firm's specialty; if not, you can tell by the nature of the sample job listings. Any employment agency listing one vice-president position after another, exclusively, is very unlikely to be interested in interviewing a recent college graduate. You can safely exclude such an agency from your search.

If you find an agency that advertises one job you think you might qualify for, by all means make a point of registering with that agency as quickly as possible. If, on the other hand, you find an agency that doesn't list any job you specifically qualify for but that does carry some advertisements that appeal to you, it would be worthwhile to visit that agency also.

EMPLOYMENT AGENCIES

No job search can be considered complete without the help of the appropriate private employment agency. By appropriate, we mean an agency that is geared toward placing recent college graduates. Obviously an agency whose expertise lies in the recruitment of certified public accounts and comptrollers would not be right for you.

You can find some valuable information right in your local classified newspaper ads or Yellow Pages.

Of course, the ideal way of finding the agency best suited to your needs is personal recommendations. Don't be afraid to ask anyone you know (working or searching like yourself) if they would be willing to give you some suggestions. You'll be surprised not only at how cooperative they will be in giving you this information, but at how many will go one step further and suggest that you use their name. Little by little, your job sources and contact list will grow larger.

It's an excellent idea to call personnel departments of some of the companies you would like to work for, and, after explaining that you're a recent graduate, ask if they could recommend a suitable employment agency. No only will you receive good suggestions, but a few of the companies may very well invite you to meet a staff member for an interview.

When you get to the agency, make sure to follow their rules. If they ask you to call to make an appointment, by all means do so; if the agency has special interviewing hours, be sure to visit during those hours; if they ask you to fill out an application *even though you have a résumé*, do so (there are some very valid reasons for this, by the way!). Don't balk, complain, or question. *Simply cooperate.*

A private employment agency has just one source of income—that is earning fees by getting people jobs. Therefore, an agency has more than a casual interest in helping you to find a job, and, if used correctly, can become a powerful ally in your search. Registering with an agency is equivalent to applying for a number and a variety of jobs.

Your counselor will want to know what kind of job you are interested in and what your salary minimum is. He or she will be a good judge of whether your aspirations are realistic and might suggest certain compromises. Listen with an open mind. Counselors are very much in touch with employers' needs and have a finger on the pulse of the job market.

After establishing rapport, your placement counselor or manager (as they are often called) will describe those openings that will interest you and for which you are qualified. You are under no obligation to go to all—or any—of the companies suggested. You make the choice and the counselor will make only those referrals.

Go on as many interviews as you possibly can. We've had considerable experience in referring college grads to a "mediocre-sounding" job with a good company and being pleasantly surprised at the outcome. The applicants would go with the feeling that, though the jobs didn't sound that special, they would benefit from the experience of being interviewed, and if they created a good impression, they might be considered for job openings sometime in the future. The candidates were pleased and surprised to find that the interview resulted in a job offer—not the one they were referred to but a much more interesting position that had just become available.

If, after the first interview with the agency, none of the jobs described is suitable, you will be kept on file and considered for every new opening that arises. Effectively, the agency does the legwork for you and will keep you informed on each new position. Most agencies expect and need several copies of your résumé, and you should be prepared to supply them.

Some counselors like their applicants to call once a week to "check in" to see if anything has developed. Others prefer not to be called—*they* will call when they have something to discuss. It's a good idea to ask your counselor if he or she prefers to be called and, if so, how often.

Agencies charge a fee for their services. This fee is almost always paid by the employer, but in very rare cases it may be paid by the employee (but only in the event that the agency finds you a job that you have willingly accepted), or the fee may be reimbursed by the employer. That means the applicant will pay the fee if the agency's referral results in both a job offer and an acceptance. Usually the fee is expected to be paid in six installments, and after either three months, six months or one year, the employer reimburses the fee to its new employee. Whatever the arrangements, it is imperative that you completely understand the terms. It is important that you read the contract, if there is one, and answer any questions regarding your obligation before you sign the contract.

As with any business arrangement, it is of utmost importance that you have a clear understanding of your legal obligation at the beginning of the relationship.

Don't be surprised if you are *not* asked to sign a contract. Many agencies that work *only* on positions where the employer pays the fee don't expect their applicants to sign any contract.

To learn of employment agencies in your area, you can contact The National Association of Personnel Services at 3133 Mount Vernon Avenue, Alexandria, Virginia 22305 (703-684-0180).

STATE EMPLOYMENT AGENCIES

No matter what part of the country you live in, you can register with the United States Employment Service or one of its affiliates. The state agencies operate over 2,500 local offices to serve persons seeking employment and employers trying to recruit new employees. The services of the state agencies are very similar to those of private agencies, with the exception that government agencies charge no fee to either the employer or the applicant. Their functions are supported by the government.

Every serious job seeker should visit the local government employment office. They very often are a fine source of job leads. Like private
employment agencies, the counselors at state employment offices are very
knowledgeable about government jobs, and they will be glad to share this
information with you. They will be happy to answer any questions about
market conditions in your area, available government jobs, or anything
you feel would help you in your job search.

GOVERNMENT JOBS

There are some tremendous opportunities for those who join forces with
the government and become one of its employees. The government will
continue to recruit and, in all probability, will remain the largest employer in the country. The U.S. government employs over 17 million Ameri-
cans. One out of every six employed people serves either federal, state, or
local governments. The federal government employs 2.8 million, state
governments 4 million, and local government agencies over 8 million.
U.S. government agencies hire 13,000 to 18,000 recent college graduates a
year. These figures represent a very significant percentage of our work
force and, therefore, every job seeker should seriously consider a government job.

The range of job offerings is staggering. Doctors, dentists, vet-
erinarians, attorneys, secretaries, and clerks are hired by the government,
as well as pilots, teachers, economists, engineers, gardeners, and chauf-
feurs. Think of any job classification, and you can safely bet the government hires people in that category.

Almost anyone employed by the government will tell you that they are
the recipient of the best benefits: government jobs offer the most security
(even in this recent recession, the government did not lay off as large a
percentage of employees as industry), the most superior health plans, the
most liberal vacations, and the most extensive retirement plans.

The government depends heavily on testing. Certain educational and
experience requirements must be met in order to *apply* for a specific job.
Only if you have the necessary requirements will you be entitled to take
the examination for the job. The exam is both determinative and competitive. That is, you must achieve a certain grade in order to be eligible for the
job, but the job will be offered first to the person achieving the highest
score on the test. Depending upon what job a candidate might be applying
for, the test may be written, practical, or physical.

Obviously different strengths must be measured if one is being tested
for a state police officer or a laboratory assistant. Should you take the test
for a government job and not score high enough—for the one you are
tested for or for any immediate openings—you may be eligible for a job
that will open in the future.

If you are interested in government employment, be prepared for a
very methodical search in seeking it out.

Unfortunately, there is no single office that takes care of federal, state, county, and municipal employment; each has to be applied for in its appropriate office.

For municipal employment call your city or town hall and you will be told where to go and whom to see.

For county employment call your county center (listed in your local phone book) and you will be given the appropriate information.

For state government check the phone book to see if there is an office of the State Civil Service Commission (or Personnel Board). Then write to the State Civil Service Commission requesting a list of current examinations and job openings. You should also ask to be put on their regular mailing list, as you will then obtain updated information.

For federal civil service, the main post office in your town will have some information on openings and examinations in the federal civil service.

However, to get more complete information about these jobs, you should write to the main office in Washington, D.C. Request that you be put on their regular mailing list. Many people are unaware that government jobs are available abroad as well as within the United States.

Government jobs have much to offer and, if you are interested, stay with it. Read all the literature available; your local library is a fine source. Take all the tests for which you are eligible. Barron's publishes several books that are a *must* for anyone interested in a government career. I highly recommend that publisher's *How to Prepare for Civil Service Examinations* and *Working for America*.

As with anything else worthwhile, landing a government job takes perserverance. But the potential rewards and opportunities make the effort absolutely worthwhile.

COLLEGE PLACEMENT BUREAUS

Very few college graduates really make full use of their placement bureaus. The average graduate visits it once, has a brief chat with the director, goes out on any interviews suggested (if there is an interview suggested) and waits to hear about any positions that might become available. Candidates assume that if they haven't heard from the bureau, it simply means there are no new job openings.

But placement bureaus, like everything else, are run by people who are fallible. Application cards are misplaced; interviewers may mistakenly believe that you've already gotten a job.

If you haven't heard from your placement bureau, make another visit, bring more résumés, and spend enough time with the interviewer to make sure he or she remembers you. Don't be afraid to seem aggressive; remember, this is an important personality trait when looking for a job.

TEMPORARY SERVICES

It seems paradoxical to suggest to job seekers looking for a *permanent* job that they should consider the possibility of working as a "temp." This is often the fastest method of getting an offer for a permanent position. Although services supplying temporary workers do not consider themselves purveyors of jobs, their serendipitous rate of placement is high.

If you consider the dynamics of the temporary industry it is easy to see the logic of this. Very often employers "rent" a temporary when there is a project that must get done and, for whatever reasons, their staff cannot finish it in the assigned time. Usually this happens when the company is understaffed, and not until this time are they aware that they need additional personnel.

As soon as the temp has arrived and the work flow continues, the company becomes involved in recruiting a new employee. Quite often, our agency has found that while our permanent division is screening for a specific job, our temporary division has sent a temp to cover the position until it is filled. We have become accustomed to learning that the temp was hired on a permanent basis.

It makes sense. While temps are often hired to provide extra work force during an occasional surge in a company's load or to fill in for a sick or vacationing employee, they are also called in to keep the work from piling up on a desk that has unexpectedly become vacant. While the original intention is to interview other people to fill the job, the temp is on the spot, becoming a person the staff knows (rather than just another candidate) and has demonstrated a capability for getting the job done. It is always a good idea when going out as a temp to bring several résumés, and to let it be known that you are looking for a permanent job.

One of our clients, a prestigious book publisher, asked us to recruit a picture researcher. The qualifications were very rigid: recent college graduate, art history major, American history minor, who could type 60 words per minute and had at least two summers of office experience. While we were trying to find an applicant who matched these qualifications, our temporary division referred a temp to fill in. She had just graduated from a state college with a sociology major and history minor. Her typing was only 50 words per minute (our counselor explained to the client that her typing was extremely accurate, and that her speed would pick up quickly). She was bright and cooperative, and could easily handle the assignment. While our permanent division was busy trying to find an art history major with the other qualifications, the client realized that her temp could handle the position better than anyone else she had interviewed. The sociology major was offered the job at a higher salary than she was making as a temp. We've seen temporary figure clerks offered positions as media trainees. We've seen typists become research associates, gal/guy Fridays turn into account executive trainees. We've seen a file clerk become a social secretary to an ambassador. It takes imagination, guts, and a willingness to consider each temporary assignment an adventure.

On any temporary assignment, always make a point of working just a little harder. Try to come up with new and more efficient ways of handling some of the routine clerical work. Always be sure to have plenty of copies of your résumé with you; these people are people with contacts and most are eager to be helpful.

Temporary services can be especially advantageous to beginners or to persons who are not yet sure where their interests lie. Temporary work lets you experiment by spending a few days in one industry, perhaps a week or two in an art gallery, a month in publishing and then a stint in a brokerage firm. It is a unique way of seeing how various fields work from the inside, while helping you to collect information for a wise and considered career choice.

Working on a temporary assignment brings no guarantee of a permanent job offer, but there is a guarantee that you'll meet a variety of people, be exposed to many different kinds of businesses and experience myriad distinctive working conditions. Most of all, you'll be getting what every job seeker needs most—experience while getting paid for it! By all means, consider temporary work as another source in your quest for a permanent job.

To learn of temporary help services in your area, check the Yellow Pages or contact the National Association of Temporary Services at 119 South St. Asaph Street, Alexandria, Virginia 22314 (703) 549-6287.

DIRECT MAIL CAMPAIGN

Executing a well-planned direct mail campaign allows you to take control of your job hunt. Your situation changes from passively sending your résumé to any lead advertised to actively deciding whom you want your future employer to be, and then setting the wheels in motion for that to become an actuality.

The first thing you must do is compile the list of companies you would want to be employed by. In other words, target who will receive the letter and delete any organization that for one reason or another doesn't interest you.

Bear in mind that each of these companies will be sent an individually typed cover letter along with your résumé. As an entry-level college graduate, your mailing should be sent to the personnel manager of the company. The spelling of his or her name as well as the spelling of the company name must be absolutely accurate—otherwise it will be discarded.

Fortunately all of this information is available in the reference room of your local library, and your librarian is bound to be helpful. Usually reference books cannot be taken from the library but you will be completely welcome to spend as much time as necessary to prepare a list.

Your field of interest will determine which source of information is appropriate for you.

For example,
if you are interested in:	*Directory:*
General business	Standard & Poor's
Publishing	Literary Market Place
Advertising	Standard Rate and Data
Banking and finance	Moody's Banking and Finance Manual
	Rand McNally International Banking Manual
Law	Martindale Hubbell Directory

Copy all the information correctly—person in charge of personnel, name of personnel manager, name and address of company, zip code. In all probability, the personnel manager's name will be listed in the directory, but if not, you can simply call the company and ask for the name and spelling. If the company is out of town and it is impossible to get the name of the personnel manager, you can address it to Personnel Director.

The list should not be too long. You don't want to involve yourself in an interminable project that becomes so overwhelming that you give up in frustration. If you are willing to relocate, do not hesitate to write to companies at a distance from your home. Most companies faced with a really "hot" candidate will pay for the applicant's trip to their main office. As we said before, if you are willing to relocate, it should be stated on your résumé.

Your cover letter should be brief and written in a conversational tone; avoid being pompous or "cute."

It should be set up in the usual business form and each letter must be individually typed. It should never be longer than one page and should contain three or four short paragraphs. You may reproduce your résumé but never your cover letter. The letter should be centered correctly, with sufficient margins all around to present an attractive appearance.

Start by saying that you are enclosing your résumé and would like to be considered for an entry-level position with that company. (This information concludes paragraph 1.)

Paragraph 2 should include a short statement indicating why you think your qualifications should interest the company and why you would like to be employed by them. If possible, refer to something in your résumé that will be of interest to your reader. You might point out some appropriate information in your educational history (perhaps your major or minor) or in your summer experience. You could mention the one summer you spent as a clerical assistant in a public relations firm. If you're sending your résumé to a group of organizations involved with journalism, you might elaborate on this job and mention that you wrote press releases, worked on feature stories, and assisted in speechwriting.

Your third and final paragraph should state that you'll call in a few days to arrange for an interview. *Don't wait for them to call!* As we've said before, you become the active member when you're conducting your direct mail campaign—there are certain shots you can call. Remember, the closer you get to actual personal contact, the closer you get to a job offer.

Don't be surprised if you find that your direct mail campaign becomes more expensive than you anticipated. It is true that direct mail involves the cost of reproduction of résumés, stationery, phone calls, postage—and time. But every other method involves as much, if not more, time. Think of time spent pounding the pavement, and the countless hours waiting in reception rooms for an interview. The very dynamics of making the rounds in a job search include expenses of carfare, lunches, phone calls and the inevitable, continual cups of coffee. The job hunt will cost a certain amount of money; but the investment is minimal when you consider that the rewards include not only the start of a lifetime career but a guaranteed salary that will allow you to become a mature, independent person.

7
THE COVER LETTER

It's important to know how to write an attention-getting letter. Though job hunters in general are very aware of the vital role a well-executed résumé plays in their job campaign, few realize the importance of the cover letter.

A cover letter should be included every time you send out your résumé to a prospective employer or to anybody involved in helping you find a job. While your résumé contains all the information about your education, experience, skills and special talents, the cover letter is not only an indication of courtesy and a professional approach to job hunting, but tells *why* you are sending your résumé to that particular person.

The person who receives your résumé may be recruiting for a number of openings, each requiring a different level of experience, education and abilities. Without the cover letter to tell *why* you sent your résumé and *what* kind of job you think you are qualified for, you are basically asking the reader to spend extra time reading your résumé and from it *inferring* where you might be of interest to the employer. Since everyone is pressed for time and résumés arrive by the hundreds, the probability is that those résumés sent without cover letters will simply be discarded.

Whether you are sending your résumé to answer a company ad, to an employment agency, at the suggestion of a friend, or as part of your personal direct mail campaign, the cover letter will always follow the same simple rules.

1. It should be brief—never more than one page.
2. It should be addressed to a particular individual within a department in the company, preferably by name. If you cannot ascertain the name, the letter should be addressed to the Personnel Director (by his or her name, if possible).
3. It should consist of two or three paragraphs.
4. It should be individually typed; unlike your résumé, it *must never be reproduced.*
5. You should use quality stationery; personal business-style stationery is always appropriate.
6. It should be laid out typographically so it is balanced on the page and should conform to the standards of business correspondence.

The first paragraph of the cover letter should tell why you are writing to that particular company. If it is in answer to an ad, say so, and include the name and date of the publication where the ad appeared.

If you are writing at the suggestion of another person, be sure to name and identify the person who has made the suggestion. If the person was one of your professors at college, include this information. If he or she was someone who interviewed you at another company, be sure to include the name of *that* company and his or her job title. If that person is an employee of the company you are writing to, be sure to give the name, job title or department where employed.

As we mentioned earlier, if the letter is part of your own direct mail campaign, you should explain in two or three lines why that particular company interests you.

The following one or two paragraphs should point out the features of your résumé that could be of interest to your correspondent. Since you have just graduated from college, your education, part-time experiences and enthusiasm are your most marketable assets and you should be proud to refer to them. Possibly one of your extracurricular activities could demonstrate a special ability that might be of interest to the potential employer.

The closing paragraph should indicate that you hope you have created enough interest in yourself to warrant an interview and that you are looking forward to further correspondence to arrange a meeting.

There are two schools of thought on how to conclude a cover letter. Ultimately the choice is yours; it depends on what you personally feel most comfortable with.

Close 1:
Conclude by indicating that you will be following up within the next week with a phone call to the employer. In this scenario, it is up to you to call the company and ask to speak to the person to whom you addressed your mailing. If you meet with any resistance on getting through (some calls may be screened by a receptionist or secretary) simply say, "I'm following up on our correspondence."

When you reach the person, state your name and that you recently sent a résumé to his/her attention. Be polite and friendly. Before you call, make sure you do your homework so that you can say something like, "I saw in *Advertising Age* that your ad agency just landed several big accounts. I sent you my résumé because I'd like to be part of your growth. Are there any current openings I might be able to interview for?" This will give the employer the opportunity to say yes or no. If you get a yes…great! If you get a no, be sure to ask if they know of anyone else who might be hiring. Network, network, network! Being passive will get you nowhere.

Close 2:
Indicate that you look forward to hearing from the company and that you may be reached at [give your phone number]. This may seem a "softer" approach and implies that it is up to the employer to take action. Then it is

up to you to either wait for the phone to ring, or to go ahead and call the employer anyway to follow up.

You might experiment on which technique works best for you by splitting up your cover letters with both closes. Keep track of your successes in landing interviews so you can repeat the approach that generates the most positive response.

Whatever you do, make sure your cover letter is *customized* to the employer. If you're responding to an ad, indicate that you possess those qualities specifically mentioned in the advertisement. If you are targeting employers in a direct mail campaign, be sure to work in some knowledge of what the company does, what product or service they sell or an indication that you are aware of their reputation or status in the marketplace.

As your cover letter is used to highlight certain aspects of your résumé, the same résumé may be used to pursue different job opportunities in various fields. The cover letter, stressing your most appropriate skills, interests and talents, can be geared to each particular company that will be the recipient of your résumé. Calling attention to a unique qualification in your résumé not only strengthens your résumé, but it personalizes your letter and résumé and makes it apparent that you are not simply sending out form letters to accompany your résumé.

Though enclosing a cover letter requires considerable effort, the time spent is a valid investment and will greatly increase the attention your résumé receives. You will be pleased with the ultimate results.

Sample #1 — Reply to an Advertisement with a Box Number

16 Terrace Avenue
Chicago, Illinois 11625
May 3, 1992

Box Y4729
Elmira Post
189 Post Street
Elmira, New York 10629

Dear Sir/Madam:

I am replying to your advertisement in Tuesday's (May 1, 1992) *Elmira Post* for a media trainee in an advertising agency.

Your ad specified some background in economics and statistics. As you can see from my enclosed résumé, I majored in Economics and minored in Statistics, maintaining a 3.0 average. My three years of summer experience includes two summers (1990 and 1991) with Bond & Lord, a large ad agency, where I was employed as an Administrative Assistant in the Production Department.

In my junior and senior years, I was the Advertising Manager of our college newspaper and gained some actual media experience. I hope this establishes my credentials as suitable for your opening.

I will be calling you next week to learn if my background meets your needs. I greatly appreciate your consideration.

Yours truly,

Marvin Ernest

Marvin Ernest

Sample #2—Reply to Advertisement

25 Hudson Street
Cleveland, Ohio 40612
May 29, 1993

Mr. Frank Ash
Personnel Manager
W. W. Hold & Company
38 West 44th Street
New York, New York 10036

Dear Mr. Ash:

I am replying to your advertisement in Sunday's (May 28, 1993) *Plain Dealer* for an Editorial Trainee.

As you can see from my resume, I have graduated from Cornell University with a major in English. Though my long-range goals are in the area of Editorial or Production, I am realistic about the nature of entry-level jobs in publishing and think my background may be of interest to you. I type 55 wpm and also have had three summers of office experience with a manufacturing company in Cleveland, where I handled correspondence utilizing WordPerfect 5.1 on the PC. Unlike many other graduates, I have no problem coming aboard in a secretarial capacity, although I do desire growth once I prove myself and demonstrate my talents.

I plan to be in New York City next week, and will call you in hope of setting up an interview.

Looking forward to meeting you.

Cordially,

Susan Dean

Susan Dean

Sample #3 — Through Personal Contact

95 Valentine Lane
Melville, New York 11747
June 8, 1993

Ms. Jane Raymond
Personnel Director
North Bank of America
White Plains, New York 10603

Dear Ms. Raymond:

Mr. John Smith, an executive in your Manhattan office who is a friend of my father, suggested that I write to you about the possibility of an opening in your international department.

As you can see from my résumé, I am a French major with a Spanish minor and am very interested in a position where I can utilize my knowledge of languages. I have worked as an office temp for the past three summers and some of my assignments were in the banking field.

I may be reached at 516-555-7857 at your convenience. I am eager to learn of any opportunities currently available with your organization. I would like to put my talents and education to work and am confident I would do a good job for you in any entry-level capacity.

Sincerely,

John Olson

John Olson

Sample #4—Direct Mail Campaign

36 Garrity Drive
Chicago, IL 60625
April 18, 1993

Ms. Margaret Chapman
Personnel Manager
Continental Electric
Xenobia, ME 10874

Dear Ms. Chapman:

I am writing to you today in the hope that you might read my résumé and consider me for an entry-level sales position with your company.

I was very interested in the article about your company that appeared in the *New York Times Magazine* of April 1, 1993. Your policy of having a "no turnover" company complies with both my long- and short-range goals, as I am really interested in a stable career opportunity.

As you can see from my résumé, I am a Psychology Major and was president of our debating society in my senior year. I believe that both would indicate a talent for sales. I did some selling in my summer job in 1992 (Capital Books) and not only was I successful in sales, but I thoroughly enjoyed it.

I expect to be in your area the first week in May. I will call so that we can set up an interview at that time in the hope I can impress you as much as your company impressed me.

I greatly appreciate your consideration.

Sincerely yours,

Richard Francis

Richard Francis

THE
INTERVIEW

The interview has been set up. Finally all the hard work of your job campaign has paid off: you have been granted an interview. You have interested someone enough that he or she wants to see you. You know the time, the place; suddenly you have an attack of nerves. You're both eager and anxious. You feel that everything you did in your job campaign will be wasted if you can't connect the interview with a solid job offer.

How will it go? Will you be able to convince the interviewer that not only can you do the job, but indeed you are absolutely the best person they can find? All of a sudden you are not so sure. What is happening to you happens to almost every single job hunter— you're experiencing a slight case of jitters.

If you find this happening to you, don't worry. You're in good company. Whether one is interviewing for his or her first job or is 90 percent up the corporate ladder, putting oneself in the proverbial "hot seat" can be an unsettling experience. Our experience as well as that of our colleagues all over the country confirms that the great majority of job seekers find the interview one of the most stressful experiences they have encountered.

There are ways, however, of lessening the stress of the interview. The first step is to view the interview realistically. Unfortunately, most job candidates experience the interview as an acid test of their abilities and self-worth. Such an attitude is extremely anxiety-producing and is bound to draw a negative response from the interviewer.

If, however, you view the interview realistically, simply as two adult equals getting acquainted to explore the possibility of what each has to offer the other, it can be a positive, rewarding experience. Keep in mind that you and the interviewer are trying to find out if there's any way you can be beneficial to each other. Remember, always, the interview is bilateral.

The employer interviewing you is just as interested in selling the job to you as you are in selling yourself to the employer. The interviewer's job is not only to screen many applicants, but to choose the one most qualified, make a job offer and have that offer accepted. Just as you are in competition with many recent graduates, the companies recruiting are similarly competing with every other company to hire just the right person, and the interviewer is under pressure to have the candidate who is offered the job accept it. Don't be surprised if after a few questions about your abilities and goals, you suddenly find that the interviewer is no longer asking questions about you but is telling you of the tremendous advantages of working for that company and the unusual potential of the job now open.

We at the agency have come to predict which candidates will receive not one but many offers. We have analyzed what characteristics each of these candidates possesses, exactly what is the common denominator that produces success. It is, first and foremost, the ability to create a splendid first impression that projects a great deal of honesty, sincerity and enthusiasm. Given several candidates with virtually identical credentials, the job offer invariably will be made to the person who seems most interested and enthusiastic about the job.

CREATING THE RIGHT IMPRESSION

Because the very first impression you make will carry through the entire interview and greatly determine its outcome, it is imperative to create the best impression possible.

Your appearance, the way you are dressed, your attitude and the way you communicate nonverbally are basically what determine the impression you make.

How do you convey the impression of sincerity? Easy! By being honest, open and real. Be yourself. Take the attitude that the company wants to see you, and feel confident. This starts the self-fulfilling prophecy. Feel successful and chances are you will be successful.

Any form of role-playing that projects a personality other than your own is bound to lead to a disastrous interview. There is no way to predict what kind of person the employer is looking for, and if in fact you knew, it is highly unlikely that you could keep up the drama for the duration of the interview. Not only should you avoid trying to be "cool" but you should shun any persona that is not your own. Be yourself! Walking into an interview with this intention will be the first step toward losing the interview jitters. Knowing that you will be hired for your qualifications and for your personality, *just as they are,* goes a long way toward making you appear an interested and sincere prospect.

By enthusiasm, we don't mean bubbling, ingenuous radiance. On the other hand, we do not mean—very definitely do not mean—a "cool" detached attitude. Any attempt to be "cool" can easily be interpreted as boredom, apathy, or even antagonism on your part, and such attitudes inevitably lead to a rapid, and unsatisfactory, termination of the interview. A simple way of showing interest is to look back on the research you have done on the company before the interview. Furthermore, if the information you obtained on the firm impressed you favorably, it has a tendency to "psych you up," to make you want to get that particular job, and that, in itself, will come out as enthusiasm as you are interviewed. Enthusiasm indicates not only interest but a high energy level. Employers feel high-energy people not only will get the job done but will inspire staff members to "get moving." It is not unusual for employers who have interviewed several candidates referred by our agency to call us to help make the decision which person to hire. After some discussion, we always find the employer almost invariably chooses to offer the job to the person who seems most enthusiastic.

Even though we discussed it earlier, we cannot overestimate the importance of being as completely honest during your interview as you were in writing your résumé. True, it is tempting to exaggerate, distort, delete, tell a tiny white lie or half-truth, say anything to make ourselves seem a little better than we are, but anyone who does this is playing with fire. Once caught in a lie, no matter how slight, you lose all credibility and can seriously damage your reputation.

Another reason for being completely honest is that it is easier. If you depart from the truth on your job application, résumé or interview, you are putting an additional load on your memory and this will serve to increase your apprehension. The interviewer expects some nervousness on your part and usually will try to dispel it. However, if your nervousness increases as the interview continues, this can be interpreted as an indication that you are afraid of being found in a lie.

In a sense, your employment is an unspoken contract between you and the company. There is a mutual benefit both parties agree to after assessing the facts available to them. Either party would by justified in canceling this unspoken contract if the other party had falsified any of the information. If you accepted a job at a low salary because of a promise of a sizable increase after three months employment, you would feel you had been treated unfairly if you didn't get the raise when the time arrived. And, conversely, your employer is equally justified in canceling the contract if you were hired as a result of false information.

It is not merely a matter of morality; hiring and breaking in a new employee is an expensive process for a company. As we noted earlier, in addition to the clerical costs involved in setting up a personnel file, adding to the insurance roster, setting up payroll cards, etc., there is also the fact that many managers believe few employees can earn their salary until having worked for the company for at least three months. One of the functions of the personnel department of any company is the avoidance of any such unnecessary expenses. For that, among other reasons, it is best to be direct, cordial, and honest in all your replies.

Always keep in mind a feeling of equality between you and your interviewer. Being too humble or subservient is as bad as being arrogant. Never say you'll take anything; that gives an impression of desperation and furthermore, you won't take anything. (Honestly, would you really sweep the floors or file all day?) If the interviewer asks you what kind of job you are looking for, answer in terms of a job title—Accountant, Benefits Assistant, Customer Service Representative, Media Trainee, Sales or Marketing Trainee, Management Trainee. Saying "I don't know" is the kiss of death. The interviewer's response to that answer is "If you don't know, how should I know?" And the interview is quickly terminated.

Be a good listener, but feel free to ask questions. Be sure, however, that the questions are pertinent and will indicate interest in joining forces with the employer conducting the interview. Take advantage of any pause in the conversation to ask related questions yourself, to be sure you have as complete a picture as possible of the position open, the company objectives and the part you would play in them. Usually the interviewer will ask you if you have any questions. Remember, you will also be judged by what you ask.

Be careful about asking for guarantees. Asking where the job will lead cannot truthfully be answered in an interview. Only after you are employed can the employer honestly evaluate your talents and potentials. If the company offers you—a college grad—a job, you can be sure it is one with career potential. Employers are aware that college grads will not do well or stay in a dead-end job, and, not wanting unnecessary turnover, usually will only offer degree-holders those positions offering upward mobility. However, during the interview it is impossible to predict where your talents and interests can be used most fully. After you've worked in the company a short time, you and your supervisor will decide what department will offer the maximum challenge. You might find, though your heart was originally set on a career in editorial, that marketing, sales, public relations, personnel, advertising, or market research would be much more satisfying.

Always be flexible about salary and be willing to think in terms of the potential salary being offered. At the start of your career, what you can learn, where the job might lead, the chemistry between you and your supervisor and the company benefits are equally as important as the salary.

If you are offered the job, love it, and have nothing else pending, by all means accept it. However, if you have gone on other interviews and are waiting for a decision, simply tell the interviewer that you appreciate the offer and are seriously considering it, and will call in a few days with a decision.

Even if you don't get the job, you must not dismiss the interview as time wasted. As a neophyte in the job market, at least you have experienced an interview and found out that it was not as terrifying as you had anticipated. You probably did make a good impression even though you didn't land the job. It is more than likely that your résumé and application will be filed and you may be considered for another opening in the near future. This last case is a very common occurrence; at our agency we often get calls asking if an applicant we had sent to an account weeks earlier is still available for work.

Remember, the interviewer is trying very hard to find a really well-qualified, dependable person to fill the present opening. With this in mind, you must convince the interviewer that it is in the employer's best interest to hire you. You must present yourself in such a manner that the interviewer will think your assets, talents, and qualifications are far superior to those of any other candidate.

BE PREPARED

There is a skill involved in interviewing and, like any other skill, it can be learned; once acquired, it will serve you well during your working life.

Quite simply it is this: *come prepared*. Learn as much as possible about the company where you are being interviewed. If it is an ad agency, find out who their accounts are; if a publisher, what they publish: textbooks, trade books, magazines, etc. Find out the company's main products, services, or specialties. Learn who are their executives, directors or partners, the number of employees, branch offices, and any information concerning acquisitions or mergers.

This information is not as esoteric as one would believe. All of this information can be obtained in your local library. The library contains business directories covering every field. Such directories as *Standard & Poor's* (business), *Dun & Bradstreet, F & J Index of Corporations and Industries* (self-explanatory), *Martindale Hubbell* (law firms), *Literary Market Place* (publishing) and *Standard Directory of Advertising Agencies* (advertising) offer a wealth of material.

The second step of being prepared is thinking through your verbal résumé. Your verbal résumé consists of facts and information not included in the written one—such as salary requirements. It is more than likely that the interviewer will ask you about your salary requirements. When discussing your minimum salary, try to be quite open. If you know what salary is being offered, be sure your expectations are in that range. Remember, the interview is a screening process; if your minimum salary is considerably higher than the employer intends to pay, you'll automatically be eliminated as a candidate. Ironically, often the actual salary offered is quite a bit higher than the original salary listed, so it is imperative to keep in the running.

Let the interviewer know that the starting salary is not your only consideration; you're just as concerned about other conditions. You might consider a lower salary if there is a good chance for advancement, the job offers unusual challenge, or the employer is enjoying a period of rapid growth. This basic philosophy is simply: get a job offer. Only after the offer can you negotiate a higher salary.

An important step in "being prepared" or "doing your homework" is so simple that it's often overlooked. Reread your résumé. The interviewer will probably have a copy of your résumé before him or her and it is quite likely that a reference will be made to specific sections that need clarification or expansion. The interviewer might refer to one summer job, and if you haven't looked at your résumé for a time, there is a good chance you'll flounder while trying to remember which summer you worked where. Unfortunately, not having the facts at your fingertips might cause you to lose some credibility.

QUESTIONS AND ANSWERS

How often have you thought, after an exam in college, "If I knew what questions they were going to ask, I could have done better"? Because that's such a universal feeling, we asked well over a thousand personnel interviewers to tell us what kind of questions they usually ask an entry-level college grad. Though every interview is different, all will include a group of questions that you will be expected to answer in a poised, articulate manner without fumbling. The interviewer will not only be listening to your answers but will be judging your knowledge, self-confidence, poise, and ability to think quickly.

Knowing beforehand what kinds of questions are likely to be asked and thinking about the answers you'll give will be very helpful in creating a strong impression on your interview. It is a good idea to do a bit of soul-searching and develop answers to the following questions. Of course, the questions are merely representative; all will not be asked, but we can bet a few will. Say the questions out loud to a friend, spouse, relative, or even a tape recorder:

1. Where do you expect to be in five years?
2. What are your short-range goals?
3. What are your long-range goals?
4. Why did you choose _____ college or university?
5. I see you are Phi Beta Kappa; did you spend most of your time studying?
6. What did you enjoy most in your summer jobs?
7. What did you enjoy least in your summer jobs?
8. What do you consider to be your outstanding achievement?
9. Why did you have such a low average in college?
10. Do you work well under pressure?
11. How do you feel about excessive overtime?
12. Do you work well with other people?
13. Do you prefer to work alone?
14. Do you enjoy solving problems?
15. Are you willing to take a battery of tests—physical, personality, intelligence, aptitude, or psychological?
16. What do you consider your greatest strength?
17. What do you consider your greatest weakness?
18. Are you willing to relocate?
19. Are you willing to travel?
20. What was your average in high school, college, law school, medical school?
21. Did you work while you were in college?
22. How was your education financed?
23. What newspapers do you read?
24. How do you like to spend your free time?
25. Were you involved in extracurricular activities? If so, what?
26. What magazines do you read on a more or less regular basis?
27. Tell me a little about your hobbies.
28. Why do you want to work for this company?
29. What is your minimum salary?
30. What talents do you possess that you think would be beneficial to this company?
31. Can you explain what motivates you?
32. What is your definition of success?

There are no right answers to these questions. Each person will answer them differently. Don't try to figure out what would be an impressive answer and make that your own; that kind of phoniness is very obvious to an experienced interviewer and is bound to create a negative impression.

Before you can interview successfully, you must know something that everyone in personnel knows but that is rarely apparent to the uninitiated in the dynamics of the hiring process. The job offer is not usually made to the most qualified candidate or the person with the highest average, but rather to the applicant who *best creates the impression* that he or she not only can do the job very successfully but, by the demonstration of honesty and enthusiasm, will be a great asset to the company.

THE TOTAL PICTURE

Be prompt. Lateness is rude, is inconsiderate of the interviewer's time and is guaranteed to get the interview off to a bad start. It's a good idea not to overload when setting up appointments for interviews. We suggest no more than one interview in the morning and one in the afternoon. There is no way of predicting just how long an interview will last, and you shouldn't put yourself under the additional pressure of trying to keep another appointment.

Dress appropriately, which means don't overdress or underdress. Dress more or less as if you were already part of the staff.

If, however, you're applying for a job in a field such as design, publishing, art, etc., where the atmosphere is extremely informal and anything goes (jeans, overalls, etc.), you still should dress in conservative business clothes. A chemist should not apply for a position in a lab coat or a nurse in a uniform. Interviewing is serious business and one should dress appropriately.

With very few exceptions, dressing appropriately means a suit for a man, and a conservative dress or suit for a woman. Your clothes should be neat and clean, shoes polished (and comfortable; don't ever try breaking in new shoes when going out on interviews), and nails well groomed. Women should avoid using very dark or bright nail polish or heavy makeup.

DO'S AND DON'TS

There is much else to tell you, but as a college graduate you are bright enough to know the obvious. You know you shouldn't pick your teeth, file your nails, chew gum, or bite off hangnails. Advice like that you don't need; our belaboring such suggestions would be talking down to you. Below is a simplified list of the do's and don'ts of the interview.

- Don't arrange for more than one interview in the morning and one in the afternoon.
- Do be prompt at the appointed time. Arriving late is discourteous and is guaranteed to create hostility and hence an unfavorable interview. If for any reason you are delayed, phone and reschedule the interview as soon as possible.
- Do smile when you greet the interviewer. Give a firm, "connecting" handshake.

- Do greet the interviewer by name. If you don't know his or her name, ask the receptionist. Be certain that you have the correct pronunciation.
- Do fill out the application forms in their entirety even if the information asked is already in your résumé.
- Do try to appear poised and alert. Make sure your clothing, aside from being professional, is comfortable, and try to seat yourself in as relaxed a manner as possible without sprawling.
- Don't answer questions with a simple "yes" or "no." Rather, reply with a brief, concise explanation. Don't over-answer.
- Do ask questions. If there are aspects of the job that are not clear to you, ask.
- Don't try to interview the interviewer. Trying to dominate the interview may give you a feeling of self-assurance, but it won't get you the job.
- Do be sure that the interviewer is aware of your strong points in a straightforward, factual manner. Again, keep it brief.
- Don't ask at the first opportunity what the paid holidays, vacations and employee benefits are. You don't want to give the impression that your prime interest is in how little work you will be doing or what perks are in store for you. Save these questions for a second or third interview or after a job offer has been extended.
- Do be flexible. The philosophy is to get as many job offers as possible, and then choose the best.
- Don't be downhearted. The failure to get a job from an interview doesn't mean that you are a failure. There are other jobs, other interviews. Besides, you need only one job. One of our mottoes at the agency is "Discouragement is a luxury you cannot afford."
- Do be polite at all times. Should the interviewer do anything to provoke your hostility, keep it under wraps until you get out.
- Don't hide. Some people try to hide their nervousness by hiding parts of themselves. Mannerisms such as covering the mouth while talking or wearing sunglasses create negative impressions.
- Do try for eye-to-eye contact. Looking someone straight in the eye is a fine way to establish rapport. Avoiding eye contact can be interpreted as being evasive and indirect.
- Do phone soon after the interview. Saying "thank you" will help the interviewer to remember you.

You may get the offer at the interview, or it may not come until later. One week after the interview, phone back and ask if you are still "at bat." Never try to push an employer into a decision by saying you've been offered another job (unless, of course, it is true). The employer will always advise you to take the other job, even if you were being actively considered. The employer doesn't want to take the responsibility of your losing out on another offer, and if he or she thinks you are attempting to be manipulative, it will lead only to resentment—not to a job offer.

FINAL THOUGHTS

By now you know how to write an arresting, interview-getting resume; how to go about your job hunt; how to survive an interview; and how to follow up. Aside from phone calls, there are other methods of follow-up that will increase your chances of getting the job.

Remember the competition. They are probably all entry-level college graduates with pretty much the same credentials, so the employer is having a hard time making a decision. And often it really is a toss-up. The correct follow-up letter can often provide that extra push to get you in the company's door.

THE MAGIC POWER OF ENTHUSIASM

A follow-up letter can help because it provides the magic power of enthusiasm. Employment counselors usually agree that the most enthusiastic person gets the job in a toss-up.

The best way to follow up is to say "thank you." You may want to say it to the person who told you about a job, to let the person know that you appreciate the effort; or you may want to thank the interviewer, letting him or her know of your enthusiasm. The letter will keep your image fresh in the person's mind. And that's definitely a plus! Read the sample letters beginning on page 145. The first two are thank-yous, both to the interviewer and to the person who might have gotten you the interview.

Even after the fact, it pays to follow up. For example, you've been offered a job and have accepted it. But you are presently working and have just given your employer two weeks' notice. A simple confirmation, accepting the job and thanking the person who's hiring you, will reassure your immediate supervisor-to-be that he or she has made the right decision; it may also assure you of a warmer reception two weeks hence when you show up for the first day on the job.

The confirmation should be simply written. Just confirm the fact that you have accepted the job, tell how happy you are to have it, and confirm the date on which you will report to start the job.

OTHER FOLLOW-UPS

If you went on an interview and, because you were told your typing wasn't good enough, you increased your skill both in speed and accuracy, it is

very important to call the interviewer and give him or her this information. This knowledge not only will increase your qualifications but shows
unusual motivation and, again, enthusiasm.

Also, it is not unusual for a neophyte job hunter, when on an interview, to ask for a higher salary than is realistic, and thus to be eliminated
as a candidate. If you made that mistake and now would take a lower
salary, by all means call the interviewer and give him or her this new
information. It might put you back in the running and even land you the
job.

"NO THANK YOU, BUT..."

You have been offered a job, but for one reason or another you have refused
it. It's an awkward situation that can be made smoother by a follow-up
letter, especially if you are interested in working for the company, perhaps
at some future time, or maybe in some other capacity that you have
decided would better suit you.

Just let them know why you're refusing. Maybe you have accepted
another job but are unsure that it will work you satisfactorily; letting them
know this will be a way of keeping your options open. If the company was
interested enough in you to offer you a job, it is quite possible that they
will be happy to consider you for a job at some future time, providing the
situation is mutually satisfactory. In other words, you are saying, "No
thank you, but," and who knows when your letter might pay off in the
future. It's apt to make a good impression for your courtesy alone. Companies like to think they are worth your time and effort, especially when
they have extended any courtesies to you. And, of course, they are worth
it!

On page 148 is a sample to illustrate the kind of letter we recommend.
It is only a suggestion, and your particular situation, plus your ingenuity,
will dictate exactly what type of letter to write.

WHICH JOB DO I TAKE?

You've worked hard, you've spent weeks on the job hunt, and finally
you've bagged your quarry: two or three job offers. Now you have a new
problem. Your thoughts change from "How do I get a job I would like?" to
"Which job shall I accept?" If your reactions are similar to those of
thousands of college graduates our agency has placed, this sounds easy.
The one that offers the highest salary! Well, maybe yes and maybe no.
There is more to be considered than money.

As a recent college graduate your priorities are somewhat different
from someone halfway up the corporate ladder. Does this job offer actually give what you want? If the job requires relocation, do you really want
to relocate? If you are married or engaged, how would this relocation
affect that person? Have you thought about the cost of living in a different
city? Remember, to judge the worth of your salary properly, it must be
considered into the cost of living. What are the cultural activities in the

new city? And how important are they to you? Do you think you might feel uprooted? Is it easy for you to plant new seeds? If the job doesn't work out, would you be stuck in the middle of nowhere or are there other companies in the area where you might find work?

All of the above require a great deal of honest self-study, and you must be quite convinced that you really can handle relocation before actually accepting an offer. Because of that, sometimes companies offer higher salaries on hard-to-fill jobs (extremely bad locations or working conditions, or a "no potential" or dead-end job, a situation that allows for no personal growth, limited company benefits, etc.).

Think through some of your personal needs. You've just come to a large metropolis and you don't know *anybody*. You've just received two job offers. In one, the higher-paid of the two, you'll be working in a small office with one or two other people; in the other, with 7 percent less pay, you'll be a member of a large staff and have the opportunity to meet lots of people.

Since you've come to the city to start a new life, you must consider a job that offers an opportunity to expand your social life as something more valuable to you than money.

Some companies provide training programs; others are willing to pay part (or all) of the costs of any education (university courses or private schools) that will increase your skills and knowledge. How valuable is that to you? What is it worth? How will additional education help you in the future? Do any of the companies offering you a position have this policy? Certainly worth considering.

How much you can learn in a particular job should be a very serious consideration, too. Not only is your future marketability very dependent on the knowledge, skills, and know-how you gain on your first job, but you'll probably be happier in an atmosphere where you can continue to grow. Think in terms of what your college education cost in dollars and cents and now measure the value of a job where not only can you learn, but are paid for doing it. In many cases, a year's experience in a certain job is worth more than a master's degree.

Another consideration should be which company and position will be the most impressive on your resume. Not that you're thinking of changing jobs before you start, but let's face it, this is no longer an era when people stay on a job for a lifetime. People usually make at least five job changes in their working life and might even make one or two major career changes.

Be sure, when making your decision, that you have considered the importance of being happy. Our agency advises entry-level job seekers to take the job they instinctively feel good about, the job where the chemistry is "right," where they feel the most comfortable. We've found that being happy in a job guarantees better job performance and hence promotion. We've also found that most companies promote from within and will always consider their staff members before they start recruiting for a new job opportunity. We've mentioned our philosophy before, but feel it is important enough to bear repetition: "proximity is the mother of opportunity." The wrong job in the right company can quickly become the right job in the right company.

Just as job searching is a thinking process, so is job selection. There is much to think about in selecting a job offer. It is never solved by simply flipping a coin. You must try to really think about you, and in which job you think your skills, talents and special abilities will be used to the most advantage—where you will be the happiest. Don't make the mistake of "overthinking," which we guarantee will end you in confusion.

And once you make the decision, stick to it and commit yourself completely. Getting the job is the first and very important step. Your next goal should be making the job *your* job. By giving it your all and approaching it with integrity and imagination, you will change that job into a challenging career.

1792 Morton Street
Oakland, California 94610
July 8, 1992

Mr. Martin Severance
Marketing Director
Smith & Smith, Inc.
68 Meeker Street
Oakland, California 94610

Dear Mr. Severance:

I just wanted to write to you to tell you how much I enjoyed and appreciated meeting with you last Wednesday. Thank you for the time you spent with me and for considering me for the position as your assistant. The job is exactly what I am looking for. Should I get it, I will prove I have much to offer your company.

I will call next week, hoping for a positive decision.

Sincerely,

Jane Robbins

Jane Robbins

10-26 Coventry Court
Boston, MA 02145

May 6, 1993

Ms. Sheila McBride
28 Grey Place
Boston, MA 02145

Dear Sheila:

Thank you so much for referring me to Mr. Donald Moore at the Coors Research Company. He is just as nice as you described him, and he interviewed me for a job as a Market Research Trainee.

I think I made a good impression, and the job sounds fabulous. I would start as a Guy Friday and be trained to do research: exactly what I am looking for.

I'm to call Mr. Moore next week to set up a second interview. My fingers are crossed.

In any case, Sheila, I want to thank you for taking the time to give me this great lead. I'll let you know what happens as soon as I know.

Regards to your family.

Sincerely,

David

David

126 Treeview Drive
Boston, Massachusetts 22117
June 16, 1993

Ms. Diane Oxman
Media Director
Hamilton Advertising Company
Boston, Massachusetts 22117

Dear Ms. Oxman:

I am delighted to confirm my acceptance of the job as Media Assistant. I am available to start work at the time you specified, and I look forward to seeing you Monday morning, July 1.

Let me say again how happy I am about getting the job and how much I look forward to working with you. I feel it is the perfect job for me and you can be sure I expect to give it my all.

Sincerely,

Alice Greysmith

Alice Greysmith

37 Barkentine Drive
Huntington, New York 11747
August 27, 1992

Mrs. Marian Bell
Art Director
Capital Records
Rockland, Connecticut 06013

Dear Mrs. Bell:

I'm very sorry that I had to tell you that I couldn't accept your job offer as an Art Trainee. It sounded like a great opportunity, but just yesterday I accepted a position with a pattern company and I feel I must honor this commitment.

As I am not at all sure how my new job is going to work out, will you be kind enough to keep my application on file, and contact me if there is another opening in the next few months? I hope I may call on you should my position not work out.

Thank you for your offer, and again, I am sorry I have to refuse it.

Cordially,

Nancy Feldman

Nancy Feldman

APPENDIX

RECORD-KEEPING BLANKS

Keep a record of each résumé sent and note the dates of your calls and interviews, and remember your follow-up letters. Don't leave anything to memory; maintain a written record.

The simplest way of maintaining a record of your direct mail campaign, answers to classified ads, or résumés mailed through personal contacts is to make a carbon copy of each cover letter as you type it, or to keep the cover letters filed in a computer if you have one. On the copy of each letter you can note date and result of your follow-up phone call, date of interview, result of interview, and follow-up note. Keep a separate sheet—or calendar page—with dates and times of interviews noted. It would be disastrous to set up two interviews for the same time.

A second system is to set up a large sheet of paper with column headings across the top of the sheet. The information, of course, would be the same as that maintained by using carbon copies or PC files. Below is the suggested heading for each column. Separate the headings by lines drawn vertically down the full length of the sheet, and draw horizontal lines about two inches apart to separate the entries for each company. We suggest the following headings:

Résumé Mailing	Follow-Up Phone Call	Interview	Thank-you Letter
			DATE
NAME	DATE	DATE TIME	Job Offer
TITLE	RESULTS	INTERVIEWER	☐ YES ☐ NO
COMPANY		RESULTS	Confirmation or "No Thank You, But" Letter
ADDRESS			
			DATE
			☐ CONFIRMED
DATE SENT			☐ NO THANK YOU

Résumé Mailing	Follow-Up Phone Call	Interview	Thank-you Letter
			DATE _____
NAME _____	DATE _____	DATE _____ TIME _____	**Job Offer**
TITLE _____	RESULTS _____	INTERVIEWER _____	☐ YES ☐ NO
COMPANY _____	_____	RESULTS _____	**Confirmation or "No Thank You, But" Letter**
ADDRESS _____	_____	_____	
_____	_____	_____	DATE _____
_____	_____	_____	☐ CONFIRMED
DATE SENT _____	_____	_____	☐ NO THANK YOU

Résumé Mailing	Follow-Up Phone Call	Interview	Thank-you Letter
			DATE _____
NAME _____	DATE _____	DATE _____ TIME _____	**Job Offer**
TITLE _____	RESULTS _____	INTERVIEWER _____	☐ YES ☐ NO
COMPANY _____	_____	RESULTS _____	**Confirmation or "No Thank You, But" Letter**
ADDRESS _____	_____	_____	
_____	_____	_____	DATE _____
_____	_____	_____	☐ CONFIRMED
DATE SENT _____	_____	_____	☐ NO THANK YOU

Résumé Mailing	Follow-Up Phone Call	Interview	Thank-you Letter
			DATE _____
NAME _____	DATE _____	DATE _____ TIME _____	**Job Offer**
TITLE _____	RESULTS _____	INTERVIEWER _____	☐ YES ☐ NO
COMPANY _____	_____	RESULTS _____	**Confirmation or "No Thank You, But" Letter**
ADDRESS _____	_____	_____	
_____	_____	_____	DATE _____
_____	_____	_____	☐ CONFIRMED
DATE SENT _____	_____	_____	☐ NO THANK YOU

The third system involves the use of 4 × 6-inch index cards. Again, the information would be the same as in the other systems. Below is a sample layout for the card:

Mr. Richard Rowe   Mailed 3/22/93
Chief Draftsman
Systems, Inc.
424 Park Place
Buford, PA 21370

Phone Call: _____
                              (indicate date)

(Note results) _____

Interview: _____
                    (indicate date, time, and interviewer)

(Note results) _____

Thank-you Letter _____
                              (indicate date)

Job Offer _____

Confirmation or "No Thank-You, But" Letter _____
                                      (indicate date and letter type)

This system is best for a very large mailing. You might want to have the index cards printed up cheaply rather than trying to type them yourself.

Keeping a record of your job campaign is worth the effort it takes. Especially when you are involved with a large mailing, it is the only way of insuring that you will be able to keep track of which companies you have contacted and what the results were. Aside from eliminating the chances of sending a résumé to the same company twice, or of making two interview appointments for the same time, it provides a useful means of reviewing the progress of your job campaign at any given time.

JOB SEARCH CHECKLIST

Now that we have discussed the various steps to be taken in your search for the "perfect" job, and you are either ready to begin that search or are already in the midst of it, use the check-off list below to make sure that you have explored all the possible methods of job hunting.

Did you...

1. Determine that you want to begin/change your career.
2. Analyze your skills, talents, and past accomplishments.

3. Explore different fields through library research, peer discussion and employment counseling.
4. Target an objective.
5. Prepare a résumé inventory.
6. Compose a résumé and have it typed and printed.
7. Investigate help wanted ads in classified newspapers and trade journals.
8. Check out contacts.
9. Research potential employers in business reference section of local library.
10. Use an employment agency or register with a temporary help service.
11. Determine ads, companies, contacts you wish to forward your résumé to.
12. Begin direct mail campaign by writing appropriate cover letter to accompany résumé.
13. Mail résumé and cover letter to targeted list of top 25 choices.
14. Record names and maintain complete files of mailing list, including when sent, whom to, what for, and all responses.
15. Prepare for potential interviews—determine what you want to say about yourself, get necessary portfolios, etc., together, prepare/buy an appropriate interview outfit.
16. Secure the interview.
17. Interview.
18. Send follow-up thank-you note.
19. Find out how you did (telephone call).
    Negative—begin step 11 again with new targets.
    Positive—job offer.
20. Ask potential employer any questions omitted during initial interview.
21. Negotiate salary.
22. Decide which offer to accept.
23. Accept offer.
24. Embark on your "perfect job."

A WORD TO THE NEWLY EMPLOYED

A great first job can set the tone for your whole career, so don't settle; be selective. When you do accept an offer, mentally commit yourself to the job. This means that once you have a start date, get yourself in a working mindset. If you've become accustomed to late nights and sleeping in in the mornings, start your new hours *before* your first day. Get into the routine early, as lateness or being a no-show will find you quickly unemployed again.

For most grads, the hardest part of adjusting to the working world is the loss of a student's freedom. In the last four years you've probably gotten used to flexible class schedules and long semester breaks. The good news is that your first paycheck can generally make your longing for campus life dim considerably.

As the "new kid on the block," keep a low profile until you've learned to read your organization's corporate culture. Appear friendly but not too chummy until you find yourself being accepted. Watch what others do, for example, how do they refer to their supervisor (first name or by Mr./Ms.). Pay attention to office politics, since they can ultimately make or break you in any organization. If you find yourself wanting to disagree with your boss, hold off until you feel you've established a comfortable rapport and then disagree with subtlety. Do not bad-mouth your boss to your colleagues, since it is much too early to determine where their real loyalties lie.

Here are a few tips to get you through your first few weeks in your new job:

- Learn who's who (officially and unofficially)—who holds the power, who makes things happen and who is likely to create a roadblock.
- Ask questions...don't guess as to what you think is right. If you're wrong you'll look foolish and will have wasted valuable time.
- Dress appropriately. Sounds easy? It's not always so obvious. If you want to climb the corporate ladder, dress corporate even if your peers go in for more informal attire.
- Get in 10 minutes early and don't be the first one out at closing. If your boss needs you to stay late to finish a project, don't gripe; just do it. Frequently in the early stages your commitment is being tested.
- Keep your personal life at home. Limit personal calls and don't overburden your desk with family photos or childish knickknacks.
- Don't gossip, but *do* keep your ear open to the office grapevine. You'll be surprised at what you can learn!
- Take criticism without becoming defensive. Work at getting the job done to everyone's satisfaction.
- Smile. It sounds corny, but people want to associate with others who are upbeat and cheerful.
- If there's a lunchroom, ask if you can join a group already at a table. This is hard, but isolating yourself can keep you from becoming one of the gang.
- Be nice to underlings. Never appear snobbish to secretaries, receptionists, file clerks or mailroom staff. More often than not, these are the people whose services and friendship you will truly need to succeed and survive. If you appear condescending, your copies won't get copied or you won't get your phone messages—and forget that word processing you needed done.
- Learn names. Shake hands when meeting new people, and make eye contact.

- Stay organized. Keep careful files; for example, maintain folders such as:

    Memos In/Memos Out
    Correspondence In/Correspondence Out
    Current Projects
    Future Projects
    Ongoing Projects

  (Be sure to retain a copy of everything you receive and everything you send.) Maintain a card file or phone book. Write all engagements and meetings in a calendar.
- Volunteer for new assignments. Make yourself visible to people of authority. In addition, join employment-related associations to develop a network of colleagues in your field. This will help you to become well known in your business community and may eventually help you land your next job.
- Read all the promotional literature put out by your company about itself. This will help you gain a perspective on how the organization wants to be viewed by outsiders. Try to stay aware of what is written about your company in the media and other sources. It is also useful to develop a file of competitors' literature so that you know what your competition is up to.
- Last but not least, enjoy yourself. Give the job 100% and in turn learn all you can. Increase your skills, make new contacts and keep an eye open for your next step.

No one says you have to stay in a job forever. If you're happy with the company, look for ways to grow. Most firms make a practice of promoting from within. If your first job turns out to be a dud, even that can be a learning experience; next time out you'll know what possible turnoffs to keep watch for.

People who do a good job usually find that job offers come their way. This is because talented employees are valued by both the organization and the competition. Always be willing to listen should you receive a recruitment call. You never know when a bigger and brighter opportunity may happen along. We spend 73,500 hours of our lives at work. That's too much time to waste being unhappy.

We hope that your first post-college job is a good beginning to a lifetime of career success and satisfaction. Most importantly, we hope we've helped give you an understanding of what it takes to get your career off to a positive start.